LIFELONG LEARNING

LIFELONG LEARNING

*New vision, new implications, new roles for people,
organizations, nations and communities
in the 21st century*

Norman Longworth
and
W Keith Davies

The pivotal book on lifelong learning chosen for delegates to the theme
conference of the European Year of Lifelong Learning

**KOGAN
PAGE**

This book is dedicated to
Margaret, David and Jeannette, and to Moira, Simon and Carolyn
for their patience, support and understanding,
and from whom we have learned so much.

First published in 1996
Reprinted 1997

Kogan Page Limited
120 Pentonville Road
London N1 9JN

British Library Cataloguing in Publication Data
A CIP record for this book is available from the British Library.
ISBN 0 7494 1972 5

Typeset by N C Murray
Printed and bound in Great Britain by Clays Ltd, St Ives plc

Contents

Acknowledgments

Books about learning are not written unless the authors have learned from others. It would be impossible to name all those from whom we have learned over a lifetime, but some outstanding people have given us, in recent times, both inspired help and/or valuable insights into learning about learning. To these we are most grateful.

United Kingdom: John Towers, Chief Executive of the Rover Group Ltd and Chair of the World Initiative on Lifelong Learning Business Council; Barrie Oxtoby, Rover Learning Business; Professor Jack Hobbs, Sheffield Hallam University; Sir Christopher Ball, RSA; Dr Peter Combey, University of Oxford.

USA: Dr David Stewart and Dr Henry A Spille, American Council on Education; Sam and Carole Micklus and Robert Purifico, Odyssey of the Mind Inc.

Finland: Markku Markkula MP, Anders Hagstrom and Dr Leenamaija Otala, Dipoli Lifelong Learning Institute, Espoo.

Canada: Zarina Lalji and the Human Resources Development Council, organizers and supporters of the 2nd Global Conference on Lifelong Learning.

Australia: Dr Brian Stanford, Adelaide College of TAFE; Professor Philip Candy, Queensland University of Technology; Norman Bailey, Swinburne University, Melbourne.

Belgium: Lieve de Geest, General Secretary of ELLI; Jack Horgan, European Centre for Work and Society; Jose Rebelo, Human Resources Director, Petrofina; Yves Beernaert, European Commission; Raymond Georis, European Cultural Foundation; Jimmy Jamar, European Commission.

Japan: Dr Yoshihiro Yamamoto, National Institute for Educational Research; Motonari Sano, Japanese Association for Leisure/Culture Development; Professor Yukio Himiyama, Hokkaido Educational University.

UNESCO: Dr Federico Mayor, Director-General; Colin Power, Assistant Director-General; Paul Belanger and Jan Visser.

OECD: Jarl Bengtsson and Pierre Duguet.

South Africa: Dr Johan Wydemann, Higher Education Research Council; Professor David Maughan-Brown, University of Natal; Professor Chris Kapp, University of Stellenbosch.

France: Dr Robert Crane, Institut de Gestion; Alan Young and Lewis Britton, proofreaders extraordinaire.

We are also grateful to the Learning Council and the membership of the European Lifelong Learning Initiative, and to the membership of the World

Initiative on Lifelong Learning, especially to those companies on the Business Council which are making the decision to help create a worldwide organization for the development of lifelong learning. To date these are the Rover Group, British Telecom, AC Delco, Lucas Industries, TNT, British Airways, BBC Learning Services and Glaxo Wellcome. Many more will undoubtedly follow in the footsteps of these pioneers.

> Full page black and white copies of the figures contained in this book are available from the World Initiative on Lifelong Learning,
> Rue de la Concorde 60, 1050 Brussels, Belgium.
> These figures are suitable for making overhead transparencies and have full copyright permission.

European Foreword

John Towers CBE

Chief Executive, Rover Group Ltd and Chair of the Business Council, World Initiative on Lifelong Learning

As the Chief Executive of a company which has invested heavily in learning, and who knows that that investment pays off, I am very happy to write the foreword for this seminal book. We at the Rover Group Ltd are proud to be among the world's foremost 'Learning Organizations'. If that sounds strange coming from a manufacturing company, let me explain.

In the early years of this decade we decided that we needed to aspire to be a world-class company. This wasn't just a decision made to satisfy a craving for recognition. It was a hard business conclusion based on the need to survive in a highly competitive world. In order to go where we wanted to go we asked ourselves how we could get there and where our major strengths lay. The answer is the same in any company. The strength of a company lies in the strengths of its people, and if people are underachieving the company is also underachieving. And so we set out to awaken the talents and the hidden potential of the Rover workforce through a series of measures aimed at improving learning opportunities.

We established the Rover Learning Business across all divisions, a learning company within a company increasingly in need of learning, and we invested in the empowerment of the people who work for us. I am glad to say that this strategy has worked like a dream. People at Rover are infinitely more fulfilled, more mature, more committed and more prepared to take responsibility than they were five years ago. They learn more, and learn more quickly. We can unhesitatingly say that this has been created by the encouragement and provision of new learning opportunities for everyone. We are a Learning Organization, and always will be.

What we have achieved here lights the way to what can be achieved in every other sphere of life. We have taken a positive view of human potential and our associates have responded to our confidence in them. Schools, colleges, universities, professional associations – even whole nations – can learn something from our experience. Their strengths too lie in the development of their people. Their future lies in empowering them through improved learning conditions, and in putting the focus on the needs of each individual learner.

There is another imperative why learning is now a requirement for life. We live in a highly competitive world. Through constant developments in science and technology it is also a rapidly changing world. No person, organization or nation gets anywhere by standing still or by looking backwards. Like the Rover workforce, they have to be continually adapting to the world as it is, and continuously improving their perceptions and skills to cope with it. The ideal we are striving towards is a seamless system of education and employment in which flexible human beings are consistently examining their potential and consistently developing it. This is what makes people not just more employable but also more useful, contributing members of society – and gives our lives more meaning, enjoyment and fulfilment.

This is why this book is so timely. It takes these issues by the scruff of the neck and lays them bare for everyone to see and follow. It identifies the pressure points in every sector of the local, national or global community. It makes an irrefutable case for lifelong learning, because the case is indeed irrefutable. It challenges the thinker and the doer. It presents, in a non-academic way, an abundance of ideas, knowledge and suggestions to satisfy the most enquiring and active of minds. It should be read by everyone who has a thought for the future, because it defines a framework for that future.

There is another reason why I am delighted to write this foreword. One of my other responsibilities is as Chair of the Business Council of the World Initiative on Lifelong Learning, an organization dedicated to spreading the message of lifelong learning around the globe. Keith Davies and Norman Longworth are both fellow workers on that mission. With them, and with the help of other business leaders and people from education and government, I am determined to give an effective lead to the organization so that it can develop the knowledge and initiate the action projects which will make the 21st century the 'learning century'.

I believe that all thinking, caring business people should read this book and will want to join us in our lifelong learning mission.

John Towers CBE
January 1996

North American Foreword

Henry A Spille

Vice-President, American Council on Education

All over America educational, business, labour and governmental organizations are preparing to meet the challenges of the 21st century by focusing on lifelong learning. Companies are becoming 'Learning Organizations'. Cities are proclaiming themselves to be 'Cities of Learning'. Labour unions are negotiating contracts that include continuing education benefits. Professional associations are setting up task forces and work groups to study lifelong learning implications.

This trend is a welcome change. For we have tended to be long on 'lifelong learning' and 'recurrent education' reports in America but woefully short on the implementation of their recommendations.

This is one reason why in May 1994 we at the American Council on Education were greatly interested in meeting Keith Davies and Norman Longworth, two enthusiastic and determined Europeans. We liked their vision, definition and principles of lifelong learning and we shared their frustration over the lack of implementation of sound strategies. So we joined them in their quest to change the status quo. Like them, we believed that action was needed if lifelong learning is to become a reality for individuals and organizations alike.

From this first meeting came a cross-Atlantic collaboration. To begin with, we were able to help build a meeting of minds from around the world through the First Global Conference on Lifelong Learning, held in Rome in late 1994. This event, uniting almost 500 people from 50 countries, produced an amazing array of ideas and insights. Further, the varied backgrounds of the participants contributed to the development of a common purpose through a common goal – that of using learning as a solution to many of the world's, and the nations', most pressing problems. We also had a hand in writing the conference outcome, an 'Action Agenda for Lifelong Learning for the 21st Century', a seminal document containing excellent recommendations.

Now Longworth and Davies have written this book on the subject. Essentially it is about pragmatic leadership – a practical guide to focusing on the needs and motivations of the individual learner. It recognizes that progress is made through the development of our own personal potential and examines the new roles of educational, government and business organizations, and of society itself, in that developmental process. In declaring the 21st century a 'learning century', this visionary book gives a glimpse of its potential for a more stable and harmonious future. The case it makes is economic, political, social and educational, and in every aspect of these it is irrefutable.

Who should read this book? *Lifelong Learning: New Vision, New Implications, New Roles* is especially appropriate for opinion framers, decision-makers and those responsible for the development of organizations and people. It provides countless practical ideas, challenges and strategies for learning and helping. The challenge will be to implement even a small fraction of the actions that could be taken as a result of reading the book.

Finally, lifelong learning affects both developed and developing countries and every community, organization and individual – a truth that will be even more manifest in the years ahead. I am therefore pleased to recommend this book as essential reading for all Americans. I believe it presents a vision of the future for which we all should strive.

Henry A Spille
Vice-President, American Council on Education
January 1996

Introduction

Into the Learning Century

The past century has not been one in which mankind can take great pride. Two world wars of enormous ferocity and unprecedented destruction have scarred the planet, and the cruelty and ignorance displayed in more regional skirmishes sometimes tempt us to question whether humanity has learned anything of value in the past 5,000 years. But perhaps that is a harsh judgement on a century that has also brought remarkable progress in science and technology and has created the vision, or the illusion, of a superior quality of life for a greater number of people. Vision or illusion will depend on the way in which men and women of perception and imagination can understand and use the ideas, tools and techniques now available to them for the greater good of all. The conditions exist to make great strides forward in the perennial battle against ignorance and prejudice. But for this to happen the next century must be the 'learning century', 100 years of the realizing of innate human potential. An alternative scenario, in which the powerful new technologies start to control us, or are used by the few to control the many, is not an acceptable option.

A world of learning

In a world in which rapid change has become a constant, the concept of lifelong learning already seems to have amassed an impressive range of supporters. The European Commission designated 1996 as the 'European Year of Lifelong Learning'. The Organization for Economic Cooperation and Development (OECD), which has researched lifelong learning under the term 'recurrent education' for many years, has put the subject 'learning' at the forefront of its ministerial meetings. UNESCO has denoted its medium-term plan from 1995 to 1998 as 'the years of sustainable human development (lifelong learning) and peace'. The G7 Nations, in their Naples Communiqué, called for 'the development of human potential through the creation of a culture of Lifetime Learning'.

New organizations such as the European Lifelong Learning Initiative (ELLI) and the World Initiative on Lifelong Learning have been formed to widen the

1

debate and to initiate lifelong learning activities and projects in Europe and around the globe. Finland, the UK, Canada, Australia and Japan are just a few of the governments developing educational, economic and political policies and strategies around lifelong learning. Multinational companies in industry and business are becoming 'Learning Organizations' – establishing new lifelong learning procedures to give them a competitive edge, and the final report of the world's 'International Commission on Education for the 21st Century' presents lifelong learning as a central unifying theme.

So what is this phenomenon that unites such disparate agencies as governments, industrial companies, non-governmental organizations, professional associations and educational organizations in common homage? How does it differ from educational and business initiatives in the past? Why is it so important to the well-being of so many people on this planet? How can lifelong learning provide a framework for the discussion of contemporary world, national and local problems – environment, the rights of individuals and minorities, employment, demography, using technology wisely, cultural and physical vandalism – and provide potential solutions? Why are so many people, organizations and governments taking note of a concept expressed in the words of Kuan Tsu in the 3rd century BC?

'When planning for a year – sow corn. When planning for a decade – plant trees. When planning for a lifetime – train and educate men.'

Japan has taken a lead in the application of lifelong learning to everyday life. At the end of the 1980s the decision was taken at government level to interweave the principles of lifelong learning into traditional Japanese life and culture. Every ministry was asked to produce plans and programmes and to implement a series of measures whose effect would reach right across the country. The results are impressive. Lifelong learning towns and villages have grown up which hold their own festivals and fairs. Purpose-built public lifelong learning centres have appeared in more than 25 prefectures and 25 universities now have departments for lifelong learning research. There are more than 160 lifelong learning programmes for third-age people alone, and innumerable others for youth, workers and other sections of the community.

Ideas and ideals

The perceived importance of lifelong learning has led to a plethora of innovative programmes and ideas. Research into the acceptable uses of education technology is proliferating throughout Europe, North America and in the East. The learning passport, in which individuals carry with them a complete record of educational achievement, is a concept developed and working in Finland. Personal learning plans, with the connected roles of mentors and guides, have been developed by workers in some parts of European, North American and Japanese industry.

Experimentation into preferred learning styles is being carried out in European and North American universities.

Cities of Learning are springing up all around the world. In the UK, Liverpool, Glasgow, Edinburgh and Southampton now describe themselves as such. Companies in all parts of the globe take pride in their new status of Learning (as well as business) Organizations, and are using radical techniques of worker empowerment. Networks between schools, between schools and industry, between universities, between teachers and children are proliferating independently of the Internet, and that too is changing the face of communication and how we see each other. Successful, meaningful and productive partnerships between schools, universities and industry are breaking down the stereotyped views which each had of the other and are leading to cooperative and creative breakthroughs.

Learning audits, in which companies carry out surveys into past experiences in, and present and future needs for, learning among all their employees have been trialled in several companies in Europe. The results of these surveys can be discussed among all the agencies providing education in a locality and lead to the greater satisfaction of learning needs. The World Initiative on Lifelong Learning has produced an 'Action Agenda for Lifelong Learning for the 21st Century' and a 'Community Action for Lifelong Learning' (CALL) set of recommendations to be carried out by each sector of the community.

A creative century

Lifelong learning concepts will change the way in which we see our social, educational and business needs over the next 70 years. It will also change our educational structure from one based on content to one based on individual skills. In 1990 the Creative Education Foundation survey taken of the future skills requirements of the Fortune 500 list of the world's top companies produced the following – in order of importance.

1. Teamwork
2. Problem-solving
3. Interpersonal skills
4. Oral communication
5. Listening
6. Personal/career development
7. Creative thinking
8. Leadership
9. Goal setting/motivation
10. Writing
11. Organizational development
12. Computation
13. Reading

There may be some surprises here for many people. One definition of lifelong learning suggests that it is 'the development of individual human potential'. This raises interesting speculations. If the words 'education' and 'training' were replaced, wherever they occur within our infrastructures, with 'development of human potential', what new visions of learning might we find? What changes and new networks would ensue if Departments and Ministries of Education were to be renamed Departments and Ministries for the Development of Human Potential? What broader horizons about the purpose of education would emerge and how could these expand thinking into new cooperative structures between all departments – finance, social, education and industrial – into a strategy for creating a learning society in the community?

Similarly, schools would become institutes for the development of human potential, universities and colleges would become establishments for the further development of human potential and companies would become organizations for the application of human potential. And if all people put the development of their personal potential at the forefront of their lives, and at the service of others throughout their lives, what a world this would be. The process may take many years to achieve, but everyone can make a personal commitment to self-improvement at any time.

In 1982 the UK government started a Youth Training Scheme and encouraged companies to offer training places of one year, and subsequently two years according to the age of the young person. The aim of the scheme was to let young people obtain the knowledge and skills which would enable them to move into full-time work as soon as they were capable. This learning would mainly be 'on the job', with some training within the company and 13 weeks at the premises of a local training provider.

One of these programmes was implemented by a major multinational computer company and received the President's Trophy of the National Training Awards in 1987 for its innovative and perceptive approach. The IBM scheme set out to grow the whole person, not just to provide specific job-related skills. It also worked from the premise that every learner has a potential to be developed, even if an initial awareness of this is absent. So the focus of the programme was to grow personal and life skills so that the participants could take decisions about managing their own life, not just during the scheme but throughout their lives.

The basis of the scheme was the setting of four keystones, with all learning related to one or more of these. They were designed to encourage the development of each person's individual potential. Bearing in mind that the vast majority of the young people came into the programme with very few qualifications, if any, and had not been interested in learning at school, it was a formidable challenge. There had been no streaming or creaming of entry – the intake came on a first-come, first-served basis. The keystones were:

- *Survival skills:* acquiring and utilizing adult survival skills, such as basic literacy.

- *Their place in the world:* understanding the world in which they wish to work and live, determining the skills they would need, and how and where to acquire them.
- *Community:* developing a response to others in their world and in the wider community. Assessing and attaining appropriate relationship skills.
- *Personal responsibility:* understanding how to accept, initiate and complete personal responsibility for one's own learning and the development of one's own potential.

In addition to the opportunities to acquire career skills, the youngsters attended personal development courses to find out about themselves. They visited London's cardboard city, where people live in cardboard boxes out on the street. They attended hostels for the homeless and, in stark contrast, took tea at the Savoy Hotel. They were able to observe the full spectrum of society, to start to assess where they wished to be in it, and to discuss how they could help others. They attended local college courses with enthusiasm as they realized the need for skills to back them up in their working lives. It is to the eternal credit of these young people that they were able to demonstrate their innate ability both to those who had written them off and to potential employers. They had not let down the system; in the past the system had let them down in failing to respond to their individual needs for motivation.

They proved they were intelligent, competent, responsible, caring, and quite capable of running their own lives. The proof of success? In the first year, against a national success rate of 56% obtaining work at the end of their training, this scheme achieved 96% success. Nor was this a one-off piece of luck – every year for the next seven years the placement rate was 98%. Bringing out the potential of people may not be easy, but it proves that it is there if nurtured properly.

Lifelong learning is no easy panacea, though many of its applications are relevant, and a practical necessity, in the modern world. The long journey to a global learning society will take many generations, but it will not start at all unless we take the first steps now.

Norman Longworth, Eus, France, and
W Keith Davies, Chichester, UK
1996

Chapter 1

Returning to Learning: The Dawn of Understanding

'By the year 2000 everyone will need to be educated to the standard of
semi-literacy of the average college graduate. This is the minimum survival level
of the human race.'

Arthur C Clarke, *Prelude to Space*, 1963

A place for lifelong learning

It seems to many people who have spent much of their lives in education (and
that does not mean only professional educators) that there is suddenly an exciting
new vision. An eminent person from the American Council on Education who
worked on the preparation of the First Global Conference on Lifelong Learning
held in Rome in 1994 was asked what he thought lifelong learning was and why
it interested him so much. He thought for a few seconds and then said, 'As to
what it is, I cannot answer easily at this moment – but as to why, well it seems
and feels to me that it is the culmination of my 40 years work in education – it is
all coming together under the label of lifelong learning.' It's an interesting reply
in that for him it was as much a feeling, or intuition, as it was a real, carefully
worked out philosophy of education.

The UK branch of the European Lifelong Learning Initiative (UK ELLInet)
recently held an event which it called a 'hearing' to discuss what lifelong learning
meant. Business and industry, government, universities, schools and professional
associations were invited; 90–100 people attended, some to listen, some to speak.
Presentations were given about a wide diversity of lifelong learning topics –
personal learning plans, learning passports, value systems, experiential learning.
The proceedings of the day grew into an expression of cooperation, enthusiasm,
exploration and real learning. A few quotations cannot capture the essence of a
very moving (and learning) experience, but these are some of the things people
said.

'Society is in transformation and learning is a key process in that transformation.
The concept of the learning organization is too limited; the transformation is too
all-embracing.'

'Learning is about taking risks, stepping outside your own box, pushing things forward on the run.'

'Learning is the best way to grow. If you are in an environment which is not learning, the duck in front is not leading.'

'Being sacked was the best thing that ever happened to me. Now I take risks. I begin to understand myself better, I begin to say what I feel, not what I ought to say.'

One of the most surprising outcomes of the day was the number of people who mentioned the spiritual dimension – not necessarily from any religious viewpoint, but often as a humanistic concept. It was a thread that pervaded the hearing from beginning to end. This is not saying that lifelong learning is an evangelical concept. Its importance in the modern day is a very practical one, but it is perhaps a small indication that there is something more to the concept of lifelong learning than learning itself – or perhaps even lifelong – and that its extra dimensions are not always educational by origin.

The case for lifelong learning

The case for lifelong learning does not need to be strenuously argued to those who have a vision of a richer and more fulfilled future for individuals, for society and for humankind as a whole. For some, like Arthur C Clarke, quoted at the beginning of this chapter, and HG Wells, who expressed the belief that 'human history is a constant race between education and catastrophe', the main motivation for learning is the avoidance of apocalypse in the near future. As science fiction writers they have perhaps an interest in expressing their views in such terms. Nor is lifelong learning new. In 1609 Jan Comenius, a Bohemian exile living in Holland (his sin was to have preached moderation during a particularly nasty religious war) wrote in *Pampaedia*:

'Just as the whole world is a school for the whole of the human race, from the beginning of time until the very end, so the whole of a person's life is a school for every one of us, from the cradle to the grave. It is no longer enough to say with Seneca, "No age is too late to begin learning". We must say, "Every age is destined for learning, nor is a person given other goals in learning than in life itself".'

These words transcend the centuries and retain meaning in the contemporary world. The stimulus to embrace the concepts of lifelong learning comes from the opportunity to realize a true educational ideal of liberating the mind, and sometimes also the soul, from ignorance and doubt. Certainly there has recently been an exponential growth in the demand for non-vocational adult education in the developed world, and it is mirrored in the demand for formal courses of training.

Other learning philosophers, like Sir Christopher Ball of the Royal Society of Arts (RSA), take an economic view of the worth of learning. He says, 'Learning pays. Training (at its best) will make nations and their citizens wealthier, societies more effective and content, individuals freer and more able to determine their lives in the ways they choose.' In his report to the RSA on this topic (1992) he shows how, in each sector of society, arguments can be developed to prove this thesis. It brings to mind the old saying that if we think education is expensive, it is certainly less expensive than the price of ignorance. Ball argues that the only barriers to better economic performance through learning are often cultural, and sometimes political.

Or one can take a pragmatic view and put the burden of choice upon the individual. Human beings and organizations on this planet have three major choices.

- They can choose the path of hopelessness or complacency, believing that they have no influence or nothing to contribute, or that there is nothing to change.
- They can take the path of fundamentalism, paranoid nationalism or xenophobia and help create intolerance, hatred, war, homelessness and disorder.
- Or they can invest in the road of lifelong learning and take control over their own destiny, combining the skills of learning with the power of knowledge and the joy of being human and alive.

A base for lifelong learning

Whatever the rationale there is little doubt that, as we approach the third millennium AD, the education and training paradigm is changing rapidly in favour of more, better and wider. More courses, better teaching (or, more appropriately, learning) and a wider range of key interests to enable people to function in an ever more complex world.

The utilitarian, socio-economic rationale of training to carry out a specific function, or education to minimum standards for future employment at a particular age, is giving way to a much more holistic and visionary view of education as a lifelong process. The old industrial society model of education, which tends to fragment and narrow it into predetermined patterns and outcomes, is changing to the information society model, which educates for a wider and more responsible role in a democratic society. As Charles Handy puts it, 'Real learning is not what many of us grew up thinking it was. It is not simply memorizing facts, learning drills or soaking up traditional wisdom. While these activities may be important in learning, they constitute only a part of a larger process' (Handy, 1992). He goes on to describe learning as a wheel in which questions lead to ideas, which lead to the testing of those ideas to produce reflections, which in turn lead to new questions.

At this level, learning is a continuous process carried out by individuals or groups of individuals, and not something imposed from above. Examples of a better public understanding of this wider vision can be seen in the vast range of courses offered by such organizations as the University of the Third Age to those who are no longer considered to be economically useful ; one can hear it expressed in the groundswell of discontent against cuts in adult education; one can feel it intuitively in the aggregation of thousands of studies, debates and conversations; one can sense it as an idea whose time has finally arrived. Suddenly, lifelong learning is the subject of high-level conferences, media attention and government encouragement.

To a certain extent the movement to longer-term thinking is provoked by events in the world outside education and training. The ongoing debate on environment and sustainable development gives new insights into the need for holism and completeness. A similar trend is demonstrated in such newly developing subjects as the management of technology, in which the attempt to bring together hitherto separate engineering and management disciplines into a philosophical and technological coherence is rapidly gathering pace in the western world and Japan. Even in the sciences, by popular belief the most secular and factual of disciplines, the eminent physicist Fritjof Capra's recognition that our understanding of physics becomes limited by the ignorance of our arrogance, and the arrogance of our ignorance, has led to the inclusion of the concept of 'Tao' into the physics curriculum of some major universities. This breaks down the limited vision imposed by convergent thinking in the subject and expands its boundaries towards infinity.

Such new paradigms in the evolution of our view of education and training have implications for all parts of the system – schools, higher education, formal and informal systems of adult education, industry and business, teacher education – and for society as a whole. They force the issues in the debate between those who recommend a slow evolutionary adjustment to existing practice and those who advocate a more revolutionary approach in which fundamental changes of method, content and infrastructure are preferred in order to accommodate the vision of a lifelong learning future.

The world – a space for lifelong learning

The broadening of personal horizons to encompass issues and events outside of mere self-interest is often one of the most difficult learning tasks, and yet to create this in people is also the major mission of learning. While creativity, imagination and inventiveness are not necessarily rare commodities, they are unfortunately often regarded with suspicion and therefore often underemployed.

One of the seven principles which the Rover Group displays in its factories is 'Creativity and ingenuity are grossly underrated'. It is an interesting slogan for an industrial environment, and its significance will be explained in later chapters. The theme of creativity returns time and time again under the banner of lifelong learning, because it helps to stretch the mind, open up new horizons, persuading *all* individuals to confront the fact of their own unique potential and to develop it to its full. However, despite these new perceptions and values, the ideal, as usual, precedes the practice. Real obstacles to the achievement of a society committed to lifelong learning include the following.

- The forecast vast global population increase from a present five billion to an estimated eleven billion by the middle of the next century, which will put enormous strains on our planetary environmental, social, educational and political systems.
- The 'poverty of aspiration' (as Ernest Bevin called it) among a high proportion of people who remain disadvantaged economically and intellectually by the lack of mental stimulation and challenge.
- The propensity of governments to cut back on educational spending and to deprive schools particularly of the resources which would allow them to compete on equal terms with professional communicators.
- The shift to global religious fundamentalism and narrow nationalism which stifles individual thought, denies personal freedom and discourages the use of critical judgement.

All of these present formidable and powerful counter-currents in history's flow towards the creation of lifelong learning cultures. They are international problems which can only be addressed through the creative use of new learning tools and techniques and combined international action.

More positively, the new world educational order is now more constantly affirming the essential virtues of continuing education and training in the workplace. The immensely powerful potential of the new information and communications technologies on the development and delivery of education and training, both individually and in the mass, is gaining credibility. A further impetus is given by the widening role of higher and further education in many countries and the renewed acknowledgement of the value of partnerships with industry, the opening up of opportunities for the many rather than the few and, not least, the recognized importance of international cooperation.

Even business and industry, traditionally wedded to a competitive ethos, are combining transnationally, through such programmes as EuroPACE and the National Technological University, to improve access for their employees to advanced level research and education via new satellite delivery techniques. From here it is but a small step to the delivery of mass education using global telecommunications and ISDN networks.

Globalization is a fact. Industries are expanding rapidly into areas of the world which they would not have touched in cold war days. Countries of the Pacific Rim are steaming full speed ahead in an education-led dash for growth, putting enormous pressure on the older democracies in Europe and North America to improve their own educational performance in order to remain competitive.

Global television news channels bring world events into the living room. We are all experiencing the input of more and more information. The real challenge, however, is to our ability to cope with this new mental influx. Few of us have been given the skills and competencies to interpret this bombardment of ideas, facts, opinions and sensations wisely or to turn it into useful knowledge. Without this ability, the overload can have the effect of desensitizing instead of enriching us.

On the positive side, the use of telecommunications leads to the establishment of personal and electronic networks. Indeed, modern business could not survive in today's competitive world without an effective and easy-to-use internal communications system. In addition, university networks are proliferating and building wall-less international faculties, such as the European Faculty of Engineering and the United Nations University, to supplement the increasing output of the open universities.

In some continents schools are also communicating eagerly across national boundaries through such networks as Computer Pals, an Australian-based initiative, CL4K in Europe and the European Schools Network based in the Netherlands. Teachers are remarking how strongly the motivation to learn increases, and how quickly negative stereotypes break down, when children communicate with each other across cultural and country boundaries. Lifelong learning is also being enhanced through a more recent and interesting development of linking retired third-age people to make experience, knowledge and skills available more widely.

Not all of these initiatives are, or will be, continuously successful, and the short history of educational networking has already collected several casualties. One of the major imperatives in the establishment of large international programmes is the necessity for effective and enlightened management, and this skill is often in short supply in the world of education and training. But collectively they offer a dramatic increase in exposure to the wider world of learning for many people.

Brief encounters for lifelong learning

The implications of the concepts and practice of lifelong learning on organizations and individuals are, by definition, pervasive. They extend well beyond the traditional formal education systems into the thousands of interest groups which influence the thoughts and actions of people in modern society. Since modern ideas of lifelong learning constitute a new and exhilarating mixture of educational philosophy, learning strategy, economic necessity and cultural psychology, they need to be explained – in cruder terms, promoted and marketed – as a personal and organizational survival strategy for the 21st century. This has to be directed at every organization in every sector, every nation, and to every individual.

What's in it for business and industry?

Successful industry makes a large commitment to education as part of its survival strategy. It has a need constantly to train, retrain and redeploy many of its personnel in all areas and at all levels, including management and personal development, communications, technical, instructional and teaching skills, manufacturing, research and development, and marketing. Thus, concepts of the Learning Organization and worker empowerment, described in greater detail in Chapter 5, are rapidly pervading many multinational companies, though there is a long way to go in some countries and in smaller industries. In addition, educational audits are discovering new learning demands and a wish to expand horizons well beyond work-related topics. The education and training needs of all employees in a company for the foreseeable future will be provided through a combination of traditionally presented courses and the use of open and distance learning tools and techniques. Learning and personal growth for all will become incorporated into a company's continuing management and career development structure.

In the past many large companies have met most of their training needs internally. However, such are the pressures on companies that they are beginning to realize that they can no longer afford to expand their education and training functions, in spite of the constant search for educational cost-effectiveness by a heavy use of information technology. Increasingly, industry is looking to 'out-source' many of its courses to more traditional education providers, and to pare down its workforce into a core cadre of essential staff.

Small and medium-sized enterprises have always had an education and training problem. With a few exceptions they have had neither the resources to develop sophisticated in-company education and training strategies nor the contacts in further and higher education to influence content and help tailor courses to needs. They have been trapped into a strategy of seeking short-term answers to longer-term problems. However, they are increasingly understanding the need not only continuously to update their key technical and managerial staff but also to develop a longer-term strategy for all employees. They are also looking to new technology and open learning to help solve some of their needs. Professor Tom Stonier of Bradford University states in *The Wealth of Information*, 'An educated workforce learns how to exploit new technology – an ignorant one becomes its victim', and many companies still have much to do to produce an educated workforce, or perhaps even to define what that may be.

One likely outcome of the trend towards out-sourcing of continuing education is the establishment of small training companies. These will offer not only a diverse range of course content, whether it be subject or skills oriented, but also a distinct scope for choice of learning styles. In this way, one of the major goals of lifelong learning, to tailor both content and approach to the needs of the learner, can be partly realized through the application of market forces. This itself raises interesting questions about the future structure of work, in which there is a continuing need to adapt to changing demands, and about the nature of educational preparation for this.

Whither higher education?

Many influences are helping to shape the university of the future, most of them expanding its role well beyond the provision of undergraduate and postgraduate education and research in specific disciplines. They include the development and use of education technology tools and techniques, a vast increase in the number of mature students and a greater number of partnerships with industry in order to respond to 'out-sourcing'. Universities will be required to play a much larger leadership role both nationally and, more urgently, in the satisfaction of community learning requirements. Governments, of whatever colour or nationality, are likely to discourage greater central funding in favour of more investment by higher education into alternative sources of income. The provision of continuing education for industry, for local government organizations and for community needs is one such major income source.

At the same time the field of continuing education itself is undergoing development and being subsumed into the larger concept of lifelong education which, among other things, can entail periods in and out of education as an opportunity for large numbers of people. This predicates a radically different mission and way of working for many educational organizations. The immediate implications for higher and further education are readily apparent. A vastly increasing demand for advanced level education in industry represents an opportunity for increased revenue, further education/industry partnerships, participation in local and national initiatives and a new role for many faculties and departments. It also represents great change, and the opportunity to be innovative in its role as provider of this education. In accepting this challenge, however, higher and further education should be aware that industry has its own, sometimes quite different, approach to education, based on what it regards as 'quality'. This includes:

- copious use of high quality (content and presentation) support materials;
- frequent administration of educational quality measurement tools (in some cases this extends beyond the course itself into the measurement of subsequent performance on the job and eventually into a company's results);
- use of distance and open learning strategies involving a mixture of presentation methods from local, national and international sources.

It can also involve the employment of electronic networking and conferencing software to create student/student and student/staff communication forums, to develop and deliver education jointly with the company, and to access databases and information sources. On-line video delivery, with feedback facilities, to classrooms based all over the country would require special instructional techniques to master the processes and higher education would need to understand these.

European universities and colleges, like their US counterparts, are already implementing strategies involving the development of modular courses which can be delivered both to industry – at the workplace if necessary – and within the university itself. While these are currently predominantly in the engineering and scientific disciplines, there is a real opportunity here for universities to develop joint educational initiatives which include aspects of the humanities, arts and social sciences.

There is a price to be paid, of course, and universities may be the last bastion of higher and further education prepared to pay it. In the lifelong learning scenario, a university would need to reassess completely its objectives and priorities, particularly its entry requirements, its methods of working and its assessment and qualifications structures. Students of all ages may wish to access its courses at both post- and undergraduate level and use a variety of educational methodologies. Lifelong learning challenges the traditional university role as a repository of the intellectual capital of a nation and as a centre for research and excellence only. It is enough to make many higher education staff, from vice-chancellors to lecturers, shudder, but radical change is inevitably coming, and those organizations which are prepared for it will be best fitted to survive in a polyaccessible educational world.

The role of the university at the educational centre of a local and regional community needs to be taken more seriously than hitherto. Many organizations, among them schools, community groups, TV and radio stations, professional associations, industry and environmental groups, would welcome the sort of intellectual added value which a university provides in the form of an integrated and supportive network of learning opportunities. In the USA the land-grant universities have this function as a part of their charter, and many operate their own TV station to reach out into the community and encourage learning for those who cannot attend lectures on site. In other parts of the world such programmes have traditionally been left to the open universities, though others perform them with little coordination and sometimes little enthusiasm. Thus the challenge of lifelong learning for the universities is to view lifelong learning as an opportunity to expand their activities in all fields and to understand, and respond positively to, the very different needs of their new customers.

New missions for schools

Schools are key organizations in the development of a lifelong learning culture. They are responsible for the bulk of an individual's education throughout the most impressionable period of life. Values, attitudes and enthusiasms picked up here are often carried through to life's end. There are, however, many other influences on the growing child and the pubescent adolescent. For example, in the UK, children spend little more than 12% of the year in the school classroom,

15

and not much more in other countries. Other pressures come from parents, siblings and other relatives, peer groups, television, role models, neighbourhood cultures – all influencing the perceptions and values and contributing to personal expectations and aspirations. Only an exceptional and strong-minded child can break free from these emotional chains and, consequently, the deprived youngster who makes good is very much the exception rather than the rule.

Attitudes to schools and schooling differ greatly between cultures and nations. In some countries individualism, iconoclasticism and a questioning approach are tolerated as a part of the cultural heritage and as an assurance of a free, democratic right to make up one's own mind; in others the culture demands obedience, conformity and group accord. In some the teacher is an authority not to be questioned; in others enquiry is built into the system and seen as good for the maintenance of a richer, pluralistic society. Nor are these stereotypes clear-cut. In some nations the resultant adult is often the antithesis of the apparent bias in the educational system. A rigid system often produces pragmatic people and vice versa. Moreover, in many countries and regions, schools differ greatly from each other and fiercely defend their independence. Whatever the educational culture, however, every school would proclaim the idea that it is trying to inspire the lifelong learning ideal in children of all ages, and the non-achievement of so fine an objective must be the result of other, more powerful, influences. The following suggests more positively, and at a general level, what schools might do to improve the chances of imparting lifelong learning attitudes to children.

- Schools should be in a position to compete more effectively with those powerful influences, such as television, which so obviously affect children's perceptions, ideas and dreams. Teachers are not generally given the sophisticated tools and techniques of persuasion available to the media and are often under-resourced and over-extended. Class sizes of more than 20 ration the giving of individual attention into inadequate chunks, and words, whether oral or on a blackboard, do not begin to compete with moving pictures and graphics as a stimulus to learn. A lecture can be defined as a means of passing the notes of the teacher into the notes of the student without passing through the minds of either. In-service and pre-service training requires a complete overhaul in its use of modern technology and in techniques of communication. Learning *can* be a more enjoyable, exciting and more effective activity, but professional teachers have to know how to make it so.
- Those schools which participate in electronic networks to establish links between children from different cultures and countries are more likely to produce open and outward-looking children. These networks can be used innovatively and effectively as collaborative learning tools in language, geography, mathematics and other subjects. Experience has shown how greatly motivation, understanding and insight are enhanced through this medium, and only a lack of imagination acts as a barrier to the realization of

possibilities and opportunities for closer and more fruitful cooperation.

- Schools which treat children as individuals rather than groups of individuals are more likely to instil a love of learning than those which do not. This extends beyond a caring attitude, which schools in general already aspire to, into the teaching and learning process itself. Again the use of information technology allows each child to be individually challenged through multimedia software which presents powerful ideas and concepts. The potential impact of the personal computer on learning styles is akin to that of the discovery of the wheel or of fire on social habits. Personal computers, in their role of extenders of the human intellect, can act as tools to enhance the natural creativity of children, not least because their use will become pervasive as the technology becomes cheaper, more miniaturized, and increasingly accessible. The task then becomes one of harnessing and applying that creativity in a structured and disciplined way.

- Teaching children *how* to think rather than *what* to think will have a much more long-lasting effect. Schools which make learning relevant to the age in which their children live, and to the lives they will lead after they have left school, are likely to retain motivation and interest. If this means more vocationally oriented education then so be it. However, vocational skills should be taught in the context of likely future work patterns. Children need to be prepared for life as well as for work and this should be a crucial aspect of the vocational curriculum. As John Naisbitt says in *Megatrends*, 'We are moving from the specialist who is soon obsolete to the generalist who is adaptable'. Flexibility and adaptability will be high on the list of desirable attributes in the future.

- The learning of high-order understanding skills by children is more important than the assimilation of facts and information. Though the development of memory skills is important in educational development, the regurgitation of memorized information is no substitute for understanding, insight and knowledge – nor is it a reliable indicator of intelligence. The information explosion can become the ignorance explosion unless, for example, information handling, decision-making, problem-solving and thinking skills take their place alongside memory skills and study skills as priority targets.

In many countries education at schools level has tended to be an obstacle course with the emphasis on failure to overcome the hurdles set in the path towards university entrance standard. It takes little account of late development, multiple mentalities, measuring a variety of potentials, new ways and preferred styles of learning. Lifelong learning precepts imply counselling opportunities which identify, and then develop, potential. They demand the evolution of flexible, more individually goal-oriented methods of learning, and the identification of the school as a place of excitement, opportunity and enjoyment. To supplement these one can add affirmative and constructive measurement and accreditation systems.

Such changes will need time, productive effort and major cultural surgery through lifelong learning research and development.

A government for lifelong learning

'Lifelong learning will be essential for everyone as we move into the 21st century and has to be made accessible to all.' These are the opening words of the OECD report on the meetings of Ministers of Education in January 1996. Government is becoming ready to acknowledge its guiding role. Ministerial meetings of the Council of Europe, UNESCO and of other international government forums are also increasingly paying attention to lifelong learning as a means of solving unemployment problems, improving national competitiveness, giving purpose to education and training and promoting creativity and social stability. An interesting new dimension is that not only Ministers of Education, who might be expected to support such positions, but Ministers of Finance, Employment and Industry, are echoing the message.

Through its economic and political power, government is the enabler of lifelong learning programmes, values and attitudes. It has the ability to define targets, support worthwhile initiatives, change systems, influence developments and turn ideas into action. Where national government can provide encouragement and establish the means of disseminating good practice, local government can initiate new projects to make lifelong learning work in the regions. Radical measures would include tax incentives, investment grants for new technologies and ministerial committees with the remit to produce plans and to implement them.

We can learn much from Japan's experience. When each Ministry produces an annually updatable Lifelong Learning Programme there is a strong chance that these programmes will be implemented throughout the country. In all countries each age and interest group needs to be represented. There are many ways in which the more learning-backward countries can adapt ideas into their own national cultural contexts. The negative argument also applies. If countries do not implement such strategies they will fall behind in educational, social and economic terms and will lose international influence and, in the long run, their stability.

Government's main contribution is as a promoter of lifelong learning values through legislation, example, delegation, policy initiatives and creative leadership. The government which governs creatively will tend to encourage creativity in its people. It should initiate and carry out the debate openly and use the media imaginatively to make the case for lifelong learning.

Lifelong learning outside the system

A lifelong learning scenario for the future would combine the distribution of information about courses, events and activities through many channels. They would describe many topics and include many approaches to education. The benefits of learning would be positively marketed with the focus on the learner. The courses themselves would be available at learning centres, at home, at the workplace – wherever the learner wanted to take them. They would be presented in many formats, from self-study open-learning programmes using video, sound and multimedia software to traditional classrooms and public lectures. Institutions of learning – schools, universities, further education colleges, teachers' centres – would be open to all who wished to attend, whether or not they intended to take a qualifying examination at the end. However, if they did, the sum of all their experience, including their life and work experience, should be taken into account. The technology to make this dream a reality already exists.

Lifelong learning is also applicable in adult and vocational education, in programmes for the disabled and other minorities, and in every trades union and professional association with a responsibility to its membership. It influences both the general and the particular. It can address the needs of women, the poor, the disadvantaged. In order to do all these things a coherent strategy needs to be developed and implemented which integrates activities and efforts. In this way a true lifelong learning society whose characteristics are described in Figures 26 and 27 can be created (see pp 127–28).

The learning process – a new look at lifelong learning

Figure 1 shows a diagram of a new seamless requirement for lifelong learning. It encapsulates most of the hazards and opportunities in the individual's learning journey throughout life.

Along Axis A – the 'Learner' – are the lifelong learning values, skills and attributes which every learner brings to the process (whatever his or her motivation) as he/she progresses through a lifetime learning cycle shown along Axis B. Axis B is the 'Lifelong' – the different stages in the journey of life which all learners pass through as they dip into and out of formal learning systems or as they acquire knowledge and understanding through informal learning systems. Axis C is the 'Learning' – a generic list of the enabling and supporting attributes of the system which learners encounter and adapt to their own needs.

The whole forms a seamless learning system whose major administrative components are transparent to the learner and which is in place for the benefit of learners. Teachers and administrators can use it to monitor progress, decide priorities and strategies and offer genuine choice in methodology and content. Flexibility is the key. The object is not to imprison the learner within the system, but to mask those parts of the system which are irrelevant to the learner and to create a cradle-to-grave set of opportunities which can be taken up as and when the learner feels so inclined or motivated.

Lifelong education becomes a process, a continuum of interdependent elements capable of being tailored to individual need in each part of one's educational lifetime. The theme of process and its constituent parts will be taken up again in later chapters.

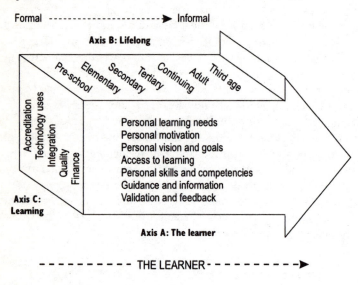

Figure 1: *The learning process*

Chapter 2

Determining Learning: What in the World is Happening?

The meaning of lifelong learning

In Chapter 1 we made a strong case for the ideas behind lifelong learning to be adopted in all aspects of life, leisure, work and family. In some countries it is often confused with continuing education, where it is for adults only, oriented towards the needs of universities and industry, and training, rather than learning, based. In others it is adult education for leisure, catering only for the needs of those who wish to take courses in self-improvement. In our view lifelong learning is much more than this. It must be both lifelong and about learning. In that context, therefore, we should now try to define the scope of lifelong learning and, from there, explore why it is so important for everyone as a concept for the rest of this century and into the next.

There are hundreds of definitions of lifelong learning, and each is appropriate to its own environment. It has a social, political, personal and an educational meaning. In the end, however, it is the individual who makes learning decisions, and personal motivation on the part of many people is the only true stimulator of learning opportunities. Everything else is the infrastructure built to satisfy the need or the longing to learn. As a working definition, the words that ELLI uses encapsulate this concept, and are shown in Figure 2. The rationale is based on the needs of individuals and the process which makes lifelong learning important to them in whatever circumstance they find themselves. From this knowledge the shape of the physical and conceptual infrastructure to satisfy those needs can be more easily identified.

In this definition, every word is chosen for its meaning and impact. Thus:

The development of human potential. Lifelong learning recognizes that each individual has a learning potential and accepts few limitations on that potential. Most barriers to progress are not based on biology or physical incapacity but on the limitations and lack of expectation we impose upon ourselves. We take an optimistic viewpoint of human capacity, based on the belief that all of us, irrespective of background, genetic make-up, environmental development, creed, colour or nationality, can make quantum leaps in the achievement of our own human potential – and that we would, if we had the opportunity, and experienced joy in so doing.

LIFELONG LEARNING IS…

the development of human potential
through a **continuously supportive process**
which **stimulates and empowers** *individuals*
to **acquire** all the **knowledge, values, skills and understanding**
they will require **throughout their lifetimes** and
to apply them with **confidence, creativity and enjoyment**
in all **roles, circumstances, and environments**.

Figure 2: *Lifelong learning – a definition*

Continuously implies that the supply of learning opportunities is constantly available and matches the demand from all who require it. In a lifelong learning world the demand itself will be high and continuous and independent of age or gender.

Supportive includes many things:

- the support of specially trained professionals – perhaps called learning counsellors;
- a welcoming and sympathetic attitude to new learners with or without learning difficulties;
- the development of a learning infrastructure to satisfy the additional needs of people;
- a non-threatening assessment and qualifications system where required by the learner;
- personal, success-oriented and easily understood procedures geared toward the needs of each learner.

Process reinforces the idea that learning is a personal activity which takes place within or without a supportive group environment, which should be the product of a holistic and seamless structure made available by external organizations (see Figure 1, p 19).

Stimulates means much more than simply 'making available' or the establishment of a 'take it or leave it' information service. It actively and positively promotes learning as a pleasurable and rewarding experience and gives the message that everyone is both eligible and welcome. The stimulation should be inherent in the system, whichever organization is initiating the learning.

Empowers puts the power in the hands of the individual to develop his/her own potential through learning – it adds learning substance to the process of 'enablement' and reinforces the concept that 'knowledge is power'. Once learners are empowered they have the capability to make decisions, solve problems, think through actions and take possession of their own lives.

Individuals – acknowledges that it is the individual who makes the decision, the individual who will make the effort and the individual who will benefit from the learning process.

Knowledge is the interpretation of information which gives it greater meaning by placing it in a learning continuum leading to wisdom (Figure 18, p 93 gives a more explicit description of this process.)

Values are perhaps the most important attributes which we can learn from the educational process. A personal value system creates those attitudes which assure a positive approach to the continuing development of individual potential through learning, and encourages people to recognize that potential. In addition to people, organizations, nations and communities also have value systems which should, but may not always, interdependent.

Skills enable learning to be turned into action. They can be equally applicable to the workplace or to social activities. The development of new skills also adds personal pride and pleasure to learning and leads to the building of self-confidence and a more positive outlook.

Understanding – the breakthrough in personal comprehension which often, but not always, results from the application of knowledge and skills. Without this learning is incomplete.

Throughout their lifetimes – from cradle to grave, from 0 to 90. Third-age communities have as much right to access to learning opportunities as has the young person at school or the worker developing skills for a job. It is not just what puts the lifelong into lifelong learning but also an extension of the right of every human being to continue to learn as long as they wish

Confidence, creativity and enjoyment will make learning a worthwhile and continuous activity whatever the rationale for doing it and whatever the background of the learner. Learning can create pleasure out of knowledge and from that comes confidence and creativity.

All roles, circumstances and environments emphasizes both the educational and social aspects of lifelong learning. It covers both leisure and work, old and young, developed and developing, gifted and 'difficult', family and friends, and emphasizes the pervasive nature of lifelong learning as a way of life rather than the restricted subset of it which we call education or training.

Our definition of lifelong learning encompasses the complete range of human experience. It is a human potential development model for the future rather than an education and training model, so inadequate for the present. Sir Christopher Ball in *Profitable Learning* gives a closer definition of learning in terms of its effect.

Learning is cumulative – we live on an inheritance of learning from the past.
Learning accelerates – its dynamic is a geometric, not an arithmetic, progression.
Learning brings change – the Renaissance changed a civilization. Today learning

is transforming an empire in Eastern Europe.

Learning pays – most nations recognize today that the duality of the education and training of its workforce is the single most important characteristic in determining economic performance.

Learning civilizes – it helps us to become effective members of our own society, to enter imaginatively into other societies and to share in the benefits of the creative genius of the human race.

Learning empowers – it creates choice. Without choice we cannot be free.

Learning is not teaching – the best teachers know that they can only stimulate the urge to learn in the learners themselves. In the future the learner has to be the focus of all education and training.

Learning is often informal – much of what we learn and value most highly is achieved without formal teaching.

Learning is lifelong – there is no such thing as initial education. Learning is as needful for adults as it is for children.

(adapted from Ball, 1992)

This is a set of learning beatitudes which might be emblazoned on the walls of every classroom, common room and workplace.

Eight global paradigm changes to bring in the learning century?

Lifelong learning is hot news now and, given its importance, will continue to be. It has stimulated several reports – most notably that from UNESCO/Club of Rome in 1979. *No Limits to Learning* was, for its time, seminal and still has much of practical use to say, even given the major political and social upheavals which have changed the nature of work, life, leisure and learning since then. Spurred by a global recession which has vastly increased unemployment in the developed world (unemployment which now seems to be structural rather than merely cyclical), the concepts of lifelong learning have taken on greater urgency and are becoming agents of survival for millions of people and a large number of organizations.

In the developing world, where unemployment has been endemic for many years, the stimulus is different but nonetheless real and active. The globalization of industry, the maintenance of minimum standards of living in the face of population explosions, the awakening of a new militancy between the haves of the north and the have-nots of the south all play their part in making the combating of ignorance through the development of human potential a key inspiration. In many parts of the globe education is experiencing a paradigm change towards putting the focus on learning, and on individual responsibility to define it, and invest in it as a means of realizing potential. Some of the many issues which contribute to this change and which increase the urgency for a lifelong learning approach are shown in Figure 3.

CHANGING PARADIGMS FOR A LIFELONG LEARNING AGE

Influence of science and technology
Restructuring of industry
Global demographics
Influence of television and other media
Changes in the nature of work
Focus on the individual
Environmental imperatives
New global power structures

Figure 3: *Changing paradigms for a lifelong learning age*

Influence of science and technology

New applications of science and technology have created an unprecedented explosion of information and knowledge throughout the world. They offer a variety of new opportunities for organizational and personal growth and also stimulate a questioning of basic values, both of which have important implications for lifelong learning. At a basic level, science and technology has helped to improve material standards of living in many parts of the world, and it has transformed our way of living, working and communicating.

The speed at which these changes have taken place has, however, outstripped the capacity of many people to cope easily with it. The wealth of information and the technology of handling it has, paradoxically, made possible greater personal decision-making and, through its sheer volume, reduced the likelihood of this being well-informed and balanced. New life skills emphasizing reflecting and thinking, studying and learning, cooperating, entrepreneurship and communicating become more crucial if people are to take best advantage of this new empowerment.

Both educational and business organizations are at the sharp end. Schools, criticized simultaneously for neglecting the basics (which themselves have changed in the new scientific world), and for not teaching the life skills which enable children to emerge as responsible adults, are often unjustly blamed for all society's ills. Higher education, criticized as remote, academic and obsessed by research, is under pressure to form partnerships with industry in order to convert new technologies into marketable products for regional or national competitive advantage. Industry is criticized for not exploiting new technology; the banks for using instant communication techniques to receive money, but conveniently forgetting these when it comes to transferring it; retailers for promoting home shopping; manufacturing industry for using robots rather than people. Conversely, the advantages in terms of quality, reliability, safety, style and quickness of delivery are not spurned. In its report on European skills shortages and competitiveness, the Industrial Research and Development Advisory Committee (IRDAC) (Commission of the EC, 1991c) stated:

> 'The relationship between education and training and industrial competitiveness is a vital one. It is changing in nature in the face of the pace of technological change and associated global competition… the education and training issues related to industrial competence and competitiveness have an overriding importance in relation to the future well-being of citizens.'

Restructuring of industry

Large industry is restructuring on a massive scale into core units and employing fewer people. The term first used is 'downsizing', the euphemism for this is 'rightsizing', and the result is called 'out-sourcing'. Professor Charles Handy, in *The Empty Raincoat*, tells of his conversations with the heads of large industries and invokes the formula: $\frac{1}{2} \times 2 \times 3$. By this he means that, in a few years' time, industries will employ half of their present workforce, pay them twice as much and obtain three times the productivity. That process is already well under way and will have a devastating effect upon existing patterns of employment. The amount of work to be done does not decrease, however, and that is the upside. Industry will close down whole departments and out-source the work they used to do to small specialized companies. Initially these may comprise the newly displaced workers, who will provide similar services to several companies.

The effect of this process on the provision of educational needs is powerful. A constantly shifting industrial and business environment gives rise to the need for education systems to develop more self-sufficient, creative and flexible people who can adapt to needs as they change and yet who can, and must, apply themselves continuously to updating their skills and knowledge in order to remain in employment. What is being described here are the skills associated with a lifelong learning perspective.

Global demographics

In the western developed world and Japan an ageing, more mobile, more multi-cultural and multi-ethnic society has the propensity to create high interracial and intergenerational social tensions. Reduced investment in welfare programmes is one result of a fall in the working, and an increase in the retired, populations. Attempts to reduce social service budgets, and to put a greater responsibility on individuals to make their own arrangements while in employment, are breaking down the concept of the welfare state.

At the same time most of these countries have experienced a massive fall in their birth rates. Figure 4 shows how birth rates in some countries of Europe fell rapidly during the late 1960s and early 1970s to cause a diminution in the number of people entering the work market in the mid-1990s. Similar figures apply to most of the other advanced nations.

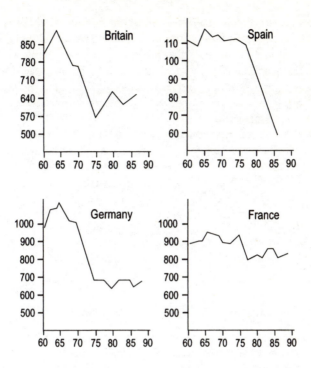

Figure 4: *Live births in selected countries*

Youth unemployment in these countries is also high, indicating that other factors are at work, among them the failure of education systems to give appropriate skills and values to those entering the job market. This is causing concern beyond educational circles. The European Round Table of Industrialists (ERT), an association representing the 42 largest companies in Europe, in *Education and European Competence* says:

> 'The demography of the European workforce is changing and the working population is ageing rapidly. European scientists are, on average, 10–20 years older than their Asian counterparts. One of the most important alternatives available to Europe is to update older professionals by retraining them and upgrading their competence. Lifelong learning should be adopted by modern Europe.'

The IRDAC report on European skills shortages agrees:

> 'the demographic evolution of the European population is such that, by the Year 2000, the number of retirements will overtake new entrants into the workforce. The ageing of the population will also mean that Europe will have to compete with countries which have a much younger workforce, will be more up to date and probably more highly qualified.'

Since North America and, to a lesser extent, Japan have much the same sort of problem, the reference in both statements is to the fast-developing Pacific Rim countries – Taiwan, Singapore, Malaysia, South Korea and the slowly awakening giant, China – which are rapidly moving the centre of manufacturing industry eastwards. In many of these countries the developing culture is one of lifelong learning among its whole population, and it is that ethos which has produced such a rapid change in industrial fortune.

The other element to the demographic time bomb is that, if birth rates in the developed world are too low for comfort, those in the developing world are uncomfortably high. In the poorer parts of the world a massive population growth presents almost insoluble problems. In environmental, nutritional, educational and moral terms, they are dangerous not just for the countries themselves but through their potential to destabilize, for the rest of the world. Many of the poorer inhabitants of our planet may be destined to live at subsistence level and below unless massive ameliorative projects are initiated. To even begin to touch the problem fundamental lifelong learning principles and the use of the new development and delivery technologies will need to be emphasised.

Influence of television and other media

Television has an enormously powerful effect on people's thoughts, opinions and actions. Where it is an instrument of propaganda it can take away a basic democratic right for people to understand truth and choose for themselves, reducing them to undiscriminating accessories of the regime. Where it is used purely as an instrument of entertainment, through trivialization and ignorance of real issues, it can have an equally insidious effect on the ability of people to make informed choices. As an independent instrument of education it could reach the hearts and minds of whole populations and transform them into dynamic, well-educated and flexible lifelong learning societies. Few people are able to appreciate the difference. In a hyperdemocratic society, in which two-way communications technology can be, and is, used to obtain instant opinions on any subject from gun control to gynaecology, from single parents to single currency, there is special concern.

The issue of hyperdemocracy is an important one. Technology makes possible instant decision-making on a diverse range of complex subjects which, in reality, demand more than an instant's reflection. It also opens up decision-making to a wider range of people. In theory this is the ultimate dream of democracy. But there is a downside to this. The notion that a decision so made is better simply because more people have participated in making it is self-evidently open to question. Quite apart from its unpredictable effect on preserving the rights of minorities – an alternative view of the purpose of democracy – it requires the skills of informed and responsible decision-making and a vision which extends beyond self-interest on the part of all participants. Using technology in this way can be like putting a child in front of the control panel of a spaceship – a form of empowerment without the safety net of responsibility, knowledge or vision. On this issue there is a thin dividing line between academic or elitist pompousness and the expression of legitimate concern. Whatever the system, human affairs are often conducted by the blind for the blind.

There is evidence of progress in the positive use of television and in many countries its effective use as a learning medium is already well under way. In the USA educational TV channels abound in most states; in Europe the UK Open University has been broadcasting educational programmes in support of its text-based study guides for more than 20 years and the BBC has a well-developed television service for schools. In Finland, one of the most well-developed lifelong learning cultures of the world, the state television service has supported the delivery of continuing education programmes for industry.

The newly industrialized countries have not been slow to recognize the power of television as an instructional medium. The South Korea Educational Development Institute (KEDI) has been broadcasting programmes for schools since 1990, 'establishing a foundation for lifelong education to expand learning opportunities for self-development and to satisfy various educational needs of the public'.

An authoritarian government will discourage the use of the media to open up the minds of people and will delegate to itself the power to enforce its opinion. Those people with the mental scars of a divisive, and largely irrelevant, early educational experience will have doubts about their ability to learn, and will retreat into the escapist search for permanent media entertainment. A society confident with its own learning capacity, a broad range of horizons and a desire to create and contribute to the future will demand from its media a lifelong opportunity for greater fulfilment. These latter are those countries whose future is bright. Undoubtedly the media, especially television and the press, have a democratic right to broadcast or write what will appeal to their listeners, watchers and readers. But rights involve responsibilities, and one of the most import of these might be to transform what people want to listen to, watch or read from the trivialized, banal and often destructive to the informed, intelligent and creative. In this way they can contribute positively to the lifelong learning culture each nation will have to adopt to survive.

Changes in the nature of work

The migration of work in the advanced nations towards high added-value service industries, high skill occupations within the tertiary sector and high technology support systems is replacing traditional notions of work content. It is the movement from the industrial society, predominantly concentrating on the manufacture of goods and products and using machines as an extension of the hands, to the information society, adding value by turning information into knowledge and services and using machines as an extension of the brain.

Most forecasts for skills needs show a massive reduction in the need for semi-

and unskilled work and a consequent increase in the future demand for management, professional and administrative staff. For example, IRDAC forecasts a reduction for unskilled workers from 35% to 10% in Denmark, three million fewer in Germany and similar figures in other European countries. At the same time it forecasts an increase of 30% for managers and administrators in the UK, of 1.5 million more university graduates in Germany, and a rise of 21% in the BAC + 2 in France.

The nature of work has also changed. Take the changing skills needs in banks shown in Figure 5.

The extension of decision-making down the line and the greater responsibility being thrust upon individual shoulders highlights the need for high quality lifelong education and training in all sections of the population. Indeed if innovative programmes which match skills to jobs are not developed there is high potential for increased unrest and instability as unemployment grows and the social fabric of a nation breaks down.

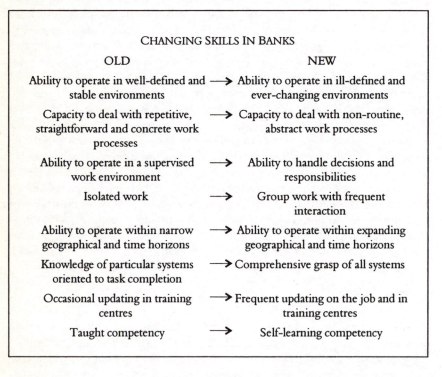

CHANGING SKILLS IN BANKS

OLD	NEW
Ability to operate in well-defined and stable environments	→ Ability to operate in ill-defined and ever-changing environments
Capacity to deal with repetitive, straightforward and concrete work processes	→ Capacity to deal with non-routine, abstract work processes
Ability to operate in a supervised work environment	→ Ability to handle decisions and responsibilities
Isolated work	→ Group work with frequent interaction
Ability to operate within narrow geographical and time horizons	→ Ability to operate within expanding geographical and time horizons
Knowledge of particular systems oriented to task completion	→ Comprehensive grasp of all systems
Occasional updating in training centres	→ Frequent updating on the job and in training centres
Taught competency	→ Self-learning competency

Figure 5: *Changing skills in banks*

Focus on the individual

Religious and family structures, traditionally the glue that keeps large and small communities together, are losing their appeal, especially to younger people. The increased focus on the individual rather than the group, and the onus to take charge of one's own life, is becoming more pressing. No matter how much we may deplore this trend and try to reverse it, it is inevitable that a higher level of education, allied to the growing number of media influences on the human psyche and the globalization of employment opportunities, will lead to a new questioning of values and beliefs, and a rejection of some of their traditional tenets. This does not necessarily mean a total rejection of childhood conditioning, but changes in lifestyles encourage alternative ways of finding meaning and fulfilment as society becomes more pluralist and offers more choices.

One corollary of this is a renewed interest by many people in psychology, philosophy and esoterica, an attempt by individuals to find themselves and their place on the planet, or in the universe. Another, more disquieting, effect is the build-up of new 'far-out' groups, often based on extremist codes and the pursuit of power through intimidation. In the face of this the need for the creative development of new philosophies and educational structures based on understanding and tolerance becomes more urgent. The development of a learning community, in which lifelong learning is a pivotal concept, would do much to provide a new, humanizing stability in the affairs of people.

Environmental imperatives

The effective management of global and local environments is imperative to human survival. In the 20th century mankind began to take out more from the planet's resources than it was putting back – more than the earth's ecosystems can tolerate for long. This is partly the result of a vastly increasing population and its demand for new artefacts, new reading materials, new energy sources. It is also the effect of the enormous increase in our technological capability, whether it be in extracting raw materials, fishing and farming, or manufacturing the goods and services required by a modern society. Nor, as we have seen, is this going to change very much. The population will continue to increase, and technology will continue to make demands on the earth's resources.

The depletion of the world's resources and the destruction of ecosystems cannot continue for much longer. It is a threat to survival, not just of human beings but of all other species on the planet. Sustainable development and the search for renewable energy sources is the very least that can be done from now on. Despite a continuous assault on individual consciousnesses by environmentalists, complacency is still rife.

There is a crucial need to educate continually the world's people in environmental matters as a basis for the survival of species. In this we must remain inventive and innovative about how environmental information is kept constantly in the forefront of popular consciousness. In other words we need a lifelong learning approach to a lifelong survival issue.

New global power structures

Empires have broken down. Isolationism, fundamentalism and nationalism are on the increase in many continents. These are the antithesis of our view of lifelong learning as the opening up of hearts and minds, but the world has to come to terms with the desire to seek certainty in familiar national or religious structures. They also tend to create a loose cannon effect. It is in no one's interest to have such former empires as the former Soviet Union and Yugoslavia in continuing turmoil and to watch idly as they turn inwards on themselves and become prey to demagogy and unstable warlords. When some of them control such terrible weapons of destruction it becomes even more urgent to find a solution. Similarly the breakdown of primitive democratic structures in other, more undeveloped parts of the world such as Rwanda, Somalia and Angola, threatens to create a knock-on effect which could eventually engulf whole continents. The same is true of ancient hatreds in the Middle East and almost anywhere in this increasingly global village where there is potential conflict.

Technical Assistance Programmes will be needed to rebuild democracy and stability in these places as a matter of world survival. An international cooperative effort to provide education and support programmes which introduce enduring democratic and economic infrastructures is also a defence against future aggression. An interesting case could be made to use defence budgets in this more positive way. The programmes should have a lifelong learning base to give them a longer-term outcome.

These eight global issues throw down challenges to life in the 21st century which only a philosophy of lifelong learning, developed from cradle to grave, can address. They are of great relevance to everyone and to all organizations, and a strong case can be made for lifelong learning, with its educational, social, economic and other rationales, being a central unifying theme of most future development. *Learning: The Treasure Within*, the final report of the International Commission on Education for the 21st Century makes just this recommendation.

Four trends for enabling lifelong learning

Four elements for the development of such a philosophy are already in place and are shown in Figure 6.

1. Increased use of education technology tools and techniques.
2. Greater use of national and international networks.
3. Development of cooperative and two-way partnerships.
4. Development of Learning Organizations and individual empowerment.

Figure 6: *Four trends for enabling lifelong learning*

1. Increased use of education technology tools and techniques

The learning demands in a lifelong learning society are huge and can only be satisfied through innovative, flexible, open and distance learning programmes. The availability of new multimedia development and presentational software enabling the combining of every presentation technique – sound, motion picture, graphics, text – makes possible a new dimension in the imaginative use of screen-based learning programmes. Interactivity confers the possibility of dialogue with the author of the learning and the opportunity to challenge personal perceptions and ideas, to become totally involved in the learning process. CD-ROM is even now obsolescent in favour of higher storage compression devices.

Learning at distance uses new delivery and feedback tools – satellite, TV, cable, ISDN and conferencing. These tools have an enormous potential to increase the provision of education and to give it a flexible, interactive, individual, lifelong learning context.

What technology provides is choice and flexibility. Research by Professor Patrick Suppé in California in the 1960s bears out the desirability of flexibility. Young people who were confronted with screen-based learning for the first time said that they preferred this 'because there ain't no one telling me what to do'. The absence of value judgements by teachers and invidious intellectual comparisons with what other, perhaps brighter, children could do, inherent in the classroom setting, was a powerful motivation to learn among less motivated students.

A lifelong learning world will be peopled by many more eager learners and traditional methods cannot possibly cope with the increased demand. Education now finds itself faced with the same problem as the banks in the 1960s. The massive increase in customers and banking activities meant that, using traditional methods, they would need to employ half the men, women and children in a country in order to cope. Clearly it was a case of automate or cry halt! They automated. Education will need to make a similar decision.

2. Greater use of national and international networks

Networks can be used in creative ways. They can help break down cultural barriers between peoples and educational barriers to learning; they can build common databases, develop collaborative teaching strategies and deliver education and training; they can assist in language learning and networks to improve communication between people of all ages. Many such networks already exist, most of them based on the Internet. But less than 5% of the world's people know about it, less than 0.05% are able to use it and less than 0.001% is used for educational purposes. Here is an opportunity for the taking. In a world which must increasingly become a cooperating global community in order to survive the future, networks can help us to promote an international outlook, cultural understanding and a global learning culture.

3. Development of cooperative and two-way partnerships

Partnerships are a recurring theme throughout this book. They are proliferating at all levels and must continue to do so for many reasons.

- Universities can no longer afford to be ivory research-only towers.
- Industry can no longer pursue profit as if separate from the rest of society.
- Schools have a responsibility to their children to bring the outside world into the curriculum.
- Professional bodies and trades unions are taking on an increasingly open, educational role.
- Governments are encouraging alternative funding sources.

Partnerships are in – from schools/industry programmes such as twinning (see Chapter 3), in which business takes an active role in the development of learning opportunities for youngsters, to university/industry joint development schemes for training and research, and international cooperation projects between industry and higher education in developed and developing nations. Partnerships are contributing to a much greater integration of all parts of local, national and global communities and, in so doing, to the creation of lifelong learning values in an integrated lifelong learning society.

4. Development of Learning Organizations and individual empowerment

Many companies are becoming Learning, as well as industrial, Organizations – another example of industry leading education in the educational field. It is also an indication of the capability of lifelong learning concepts to widen both the vision and the scope of organizations as they face an uncertain future. The twin topics of Learning Organizations and empowerment will be discussed fully in Chapters 4 and 5. Meanwhile, Figure 14 in Chapter 5 (p 75) gives a definition of the characteristics of a Learning Organization and demonstrates how different it is from the industrial society structures to which many countries and companies still adhere.

Infrastructures

This is where the most development is still needed. If lifelong learning forms an intellectual infrastructure for future development, then it needs physical and administrative infrastructures to enable it to happen. These include:

- intelligent buildings which are oriented towards the varied needs of individual learners;
- assessment, accreditation and qualification infrastructures to provide motivation and continuity;

- curriculum infrastructures to provide relevance and content;
- administrative infrastructures in universities and colleges which break down age and suitability barriers; and, above all
- visionary learning infrastructures which break down all the barriers – physical, psychological and ideological – which are put in place to prevent people from realizing their own potential.

These infrastructures need to be able to survive the test of time and funding drought and the capacity to achieve a rapid critical mass. Governments have the primary responsibility for these processes but they will need the support of organizations from all sectors of the community to implement them – and the intelligent application of pressure from an informed and concerned electorate.

A learner's charter

One of the main factors distinguishing lifelong learning from education and training is the requirement to put the focus on the learner. As a guideline for the future, a 'learner's charter' would be useful.

ELLI has developed a set of principles which could form the basis of such a charter and this is shown in Figure 7.

ELLI PRINCIPLES OF LEARNING

1. All citizens of Europe can learn and develop their human potential.
2. All citizens of Europe should have access to learning.
3. The learner is the customer and the customer's needs have first priority.
4. Guidance and support should be available to help the learner.
5. All learning styles should be recognized and catered for.
6. All learning – formal and informal – can be validated in a way appropriate to the learner.
7. Collaborative, positive support for the learner should accept no barriers.
8. Modern teaching aids should be creatively applied in support of the learner.
9. Leadership should be available for all learning requirements, levels and ages.
10. Learning should be supported through life.

Figure 7: *ELLI principles of learning*

1. All citizens can learn and develop their human potential
This is a reaffirmation of the in-built ability of everyone in a community to learn at their own appropriate level and, implicitly, to enjoy doing so. But it is not just the task of educators to develop this ability. A multidisciplinary effort of commu-

nicators, information system specialists, engineers, social scientists and administrators will be needed to energize the goal of human potential development.

2. All citizens should have access to learning
Unbiased learning opportunities should be available to everyone, wherever they live, whoever they are, whenever and whatever they wish to study. Learning should 'reach the unreached and include the excluded' (Federico Mayor, UNESCO Director-General).

3. The learner is the customer and the customer's needs have first priority
Just as a commercial organization will tailor its product, service or process to the needs of the customer and give priority to its design and production, so, in education and training, the delivering organization should take into account the needs of each individual learner as a priority in the design of the learning product, service or process. This marks a paradigm shift of emphasis from supply to demand, from the provider to the receiver.

4. Guidance and support should be available to help the learner
This indicates the need for specially trained learning counsellors to guide people through the learning maze – before, during and after their learning. Learning in the 21st century will be continuous, requiring specially trained mentors and guides and the development of individual learning plans.

5. All learning styles should be recognized and catered for
People enjoy learning in different ways. Some require a teacher, others do not, and learning systems should have the flexibility to offer people the choice. Personal learning styles are ill understood and under-funded in research terms.

6. All learning – formal and informal – can be validated in a way appropriate to the learner
Everyone has the right not to be intimidated by validation systems. Equally, everyone has the right to have his/her own progress in learning tested by a competent validation body as he/she sees fit. Intelligent validation, that which is designed to be a helpful guide in the individual's progress to self-knowledge and self-development, can be a useful tool.

7. Collaborative, positive support for the learner should accept no barriers
Everyone has the right to learn and to be supported in that right.

8. Modern learning aids should be creatively applied in support of the learner
These include modern communications technologies, international and national networks, the use of computer-based educational software, CD-ROMS, DVIs and all the other technological aids coming on stream. Their focus, however, should be on satisfying the learning needs of the individual rather than on simply giving information.

9. Leadership should be available for all learning requirements, levels and ages
This leadership must come from government ministers and officials, teachers and lecturers, administrators and technicians, each having been given the appropriate skills to understand and satisfy the learning need.

10. Learning should be supported through life
Learning should be encouraged, empowered and enabled. The third age is as important as the school age, adult education as important as vocational education.

Many of these issues resurface in other chapters, albeit in different guises. They express the sentiment of this chapter title – they are 'what in the world is happening' and they present challenges to us all.

Chapter 3

Learning Learning?
Schools – Where Lifelong Learning Begins

Handling information

A complex society like ours demands, as a basic survival skill, the ability to handle information quickly and adaptably. Both governments and industrial organizations stand or fall on their ability to analyse it, process it, interpret it, and make intelligent strategies from it. The same is no less true for schools and for people.

At the age of sixteen or so we tend to release children from a kind of bondage system in our schools into the open-endedness of an increasingly complex world. They have indeed acquired a great deal of data about many things – literature, science, geography, language (sometimes) and history, and most of them have also acquired the facility to memorize it and rewrite it onto an examination paper. However, they seem to have little understanding of what it all means, where it all fits together and how to use it effectively. It all seems to be a little irrelevant, a product of a system whose only objective is to achieve its only objective. Having acquired information in a compartmentalized way, children (and adults) have difficulty turning the data into information, the information into knowledge, let alone into the understanding which comes from putting it together into a conceptual whole. Nor do they have any love for the knowledge they have so painfully acquired. Having started in this way, the resentment and sense of failure lasts well into adult life, inhibiting the further growth and development of the enormous potential resident in all human beings.

Moreover, the schooltime preoccupation with the passing on of information inhibits the development of other desirable individual attributes. Personal value systems based on openness, flexibility, tolerance for others, are often lacking in many, perhaps the majority, though it is fair to point out that these are also the product of many influences other than the school. A knowledge of new employment patterns, sustainable development, minority rights, gender roles, personal responsibility, and the need to invest in a lifetime of learning is often conspicuous by its absence. Essential learning and navigational skills through the information society were not, it appears, on the curriculum or, if they were, were less important than the ability to commit facts, and sometimes ideas, to memory. In some countries, xenophobia is actively encouraged by its leaders through the deliberate emasculation and narrowing of the curriculum. In today's globally interdependent society, in which the toleration of others is crucial for the survival of the planet, this is worrying.

Confusion and the schools

Not that the responsibility for this should be placed wholly, or even largely, on the schools. Vastly improved communication techniques exploiting basic human psychology increase the pressure on children to adopt conflicting values and attitudes. Neither the children, nor even the teachers and parents who nurture them, have been given instruction or information on how to cope with that sort of information overload. Television presents children every evening with most powerful visual and verbal stimuli; and parents still, rightly, have the right to pass on their own truths and attitudes, whether implicitly or explicitly, to their children. Many of these attitudes regrettably are rooted in their own learning experiences, at least one generation old but often many more, and usually negative. And so the cycle goes on. Attempts to change the educational rules by which they themselves had to suffer failure are strongly resisted and fiercely resented.

Peer group pressures are also of paramount concern to the pubescent adolescent, struggling to reconcile the feel of manhood or womanhood with the taboos of home and school and the community at large. In this environment, individual learning can easily become subservient to group and leadership prejudice. The vast open world of information, communication and opportunity closes down into a series of stylized group activity options with little freedom for individual initiative.

It is small wonder that schools experience an uphill fight to grasp the attention of a clientele already punch-drunk by information and more exciting events. They have been given an impossible task by an over-expectant society. They have had donated to them, almost by default, the responsibility of widening their role in society. They have not been given the necessary resources and the authority to fulfil that role, either through the constant training and retraining of teachers, or through the increased funding which might enable them to compete with the professional mediamen.

Further, as is typical in times of stress and change, society retreats backwards into the old certainties, back to the basics, which themselves have changed and expanded so much that the old basics are no longer relevant or appropriate. Schools are pressured to adopt ever more rigid structures and curricula more appropriate to a full-employment, industrial, mid-20th (or even 19th) century environment, rather than to the new and urgent paradigm of change, information technology, lifelong learning and the post-industrial order.

How to react to these violent paradigm shifts in society, in education and in business and economics, is little understood by the vast majority of parents, and ignored, for wholly understandable reasons, by teachers and administrators. In most countries of the western world schools are encountering an increasingly strident dissatisfaction because of the schizoid personality they must present to their audiences. Those which acquiesce to the pressure to adopt a more inwardly focused stance based on perceptions of a world of unchanging values may buy themselves some short-term approval. But in the long term they are doing a disservice to their parents, to their teachers and, above all, to their children who must later experience the pain of adjusting to a world which is different in content and in kind, or of finding a means of escaping from it into a self-created fantasy.

The information society and lifelong learning

We are rapidly moving into a society dominated by the power of information – an 'information society'. Its impact will affect all of us, our lifestyles, our work styles, our leisurestyles, child and adult alike, in not more than half a generation.

Compare this with the impact of the first industrial revolution, which lasted for several generations. In this, as now, the school curriculum needed to be geared to the demands of the time, to the needs of a system which demanded the elementary ability to follow instructions at home and work for the majority and, in some countries, the much greater skill of administering an empire abroad for a sizeable elite minority. The opportunities, stresses, changes and demands created by technology in general, and information technology in particular, have changed all that quite drastically. The resultant need to be rapidly adaptable to different circumstances is a new experience and one which many people accept only reluctantly. It puts great pressure on our institutions because it demands new, arguably more democratic, systems, a high level of flexibility and versatility, and a lifetime of continuous learning.

Educational organizations and those who work within them will have to adapt in an unprecedented way to new thinking, new methods of teaching and, above all, new skills-based curricula which enable children (and adults) to accept change as a fact of life. They will need the ability to understand fully, and handle effectively, the dominant commodity of this revolution, information. Learning to cope with this becomes the key to personal and organizational survival in the information society. Effective, lifetime learning holds that key, but is constrained within an over-loaded and under-resourced formal education sector.

Unless the nettle of adopting a new lifelong learning approach is grasped, schools will continue to trail behind society's need. Nor can schools carry out what needs to be done by themselves. They are the agents of society's will and operate by consent. They have a responsibility to parents, to children, to all the members of the community in which they are situated, to the government which provides their resources, to the companies and business organizations and universities in which their issue will work and further educate themselves.

And therein lies both the challenge and the answer. For, equally, all those people and organizations have a responsibility to the schools, and to fulfil that responsibility they have to play their part in two ways.

First, they have to bring themselves up to date mentally with the fundamental needs, resources and purposes of a modern educational institution whose pupils will enter a world demanding flexibility of outlook, adaptability of mind and versatility of knowledge. To exercise their right to influence others to learn, people must also exercise the responsibility of learning themselves, of becoming seriously informed and aware of how children learn, and what they will have to learn to become rounded and contributing citizens. In a world of change they must continue to keep themselves informed about those things: thinking, thinking about and thinking through.

Second, they, as members of the community, will have a vast number of skills, knowledge and insights to contribute. Teachers, certainly in the secondary sector, are charged with giving a subset of knowledge, usually as information, within defined subject boundaries. The collective knowledge, skills, perceptions and values of a whole community is a far greater asset. This is not to devalue teachers. It is to give them a much more responsible education management role within the community as a whole and greater access to valuable additional resources.

This is one of the infrastructural elements of a lifelong learning society, in which the informal education sector – all the non-formal educational influences on children and adults, parents, governors, libraries, museums, professional societies, uniformed associations and religious organizations – plays a supportive part in opening the doors of perception for all. It has a breadth of vision which exists in very few places and which will take a long time to create. It makes the school a central focus for learning for everyone in the community, and enlarges its function. This more holistic and interdependent new educational approach can develop the skills and the knowledge which enable today's children, tomorrow's adults, to play a genuinely participative part in the society of the future.

There are other influences and other approaches. Unless they are given the mental apparatus to understand and handle information wisely, both children and adults become easily manipulatable. The ideological battle for hearts and minds waged by the extremes of our systems has never suffered from any sense of indecision or felt the need to insert balance or the right to think freely about issues. This is true whichever extreme is waging the propaganda war, and the advent of far more sophisticated instruments of information technology makes the means of manipulation so much more accessible, plausible, powerful and insidious.

The ability of the education system to maintain a wider ranging and thoughtful curriculum, to teach about such threats, about the power of the technology and the information it releases, and about how to handle both, is an obviously crucial aspect which relates as much to the survival of a free society as it does to the development of a liberated individual.

Ten characteristics for the lifelong learning school

What makes a good lifelong learning school? How can we begin the process of creating a society at ease with itself and its own capacity to learn in the longer term? How can we develop the human potential of all our children without turning them off the process of learning, and without losing the goodwill and support of the community? How can we develop children into confident, creative and contributing citizens? How do we instil the habit of learning so that children will value it as an enjoyable and personally rewarding way of passing time throughout their lives? We shall not do all this tomorrow, or the day after tomorrow, but we need to start now.

Figure 8 suggests ten characteristics by which a good lifelong learning school can be measured – that is, a school whose products we could reasonably expect to adopt positive learning attitudes throughout life.

ELLI CHARACTERISTICS OF A LIFELONG LEARNING SCHOOL

1. Has a written organizational strategy, available to all, for developing the full human potential of each student and member of staff.
2. Involves children and staff in the maintenance of a culture of quality and respect for high standards in everything it does, and in continuous improvement programmes for staff.
3. Increases the resources available to the school by harnessing the skills, talents and knowledge of governors, parents, business leaders and everyone in the community to create new learning opportunities and implement school strategies.
4. Develops a curriculum based on the enhancement of personal skills and values to improve knowledge and understanding, and enable children to manage change throughout their lives.
5. Uses modern information and communication technologies wisely across all disciplines, including the exploration of collaborative learning opportunities through networks.
6. Looks outward to the world, promoting a sense of tolerance, justice and understanding of different races, creeds and cultures in all children.
7. Stimulates home–school cooperation and involves the family in the life and work of the school.
8. Expands lifelong learning in all its children and staff by involving them in the development of personal learning plans, guides and mentors.
9. Broadens the vision of staff and children through a wide range of cultural experiences and extracurricular activities.
10. Celebrates learning frequently as a desirable, permanent and enjoyable habit for all.

Figure 8: *Ten characteristics of a lifelong learning school*

1. Has a written organizational strategy, available to all, for developing the full human potential of each student and member of staff

In industry this would be called a business plan. It would describe the organization's major goals and objectives; its marketplace and its products; how it intends to go about achieving its objectives and the resources it will need to achieve these; how it relates to the world outside of the organization; its management strategy for the empowerment of its workforce and the methods it would use to please its customers and shareholders. It would be a blueprint for action over a period of time, say five or ten years, but modifiable according to economic or other circumstance and containing checkpoints each six months or so when it would be re-examined in the light of the realities of business life. Further it would be communicated to all the people who have a stake in realizing the plan and, in a modern enterprise, they would be invited to discuss it and contribute to it.

This would seem to have little relevance to the *raison d'être* of a school. But what if the stakeholder labels are transformed into parents, governors, teachers, administrative staff, children, members of the community? A lively debate might start as to which are the shareholders, customers and workers. Who the customers are is one of the more difficult, and key, questions to be answered.

A school is ostensibly an organization for learning. Everyone there is a learner. Children, teachers and administrative staff and their learning needs are paramount. So the first priority of an organizational strategy is to put the focus of activity on the satisfaction of learning needs for each member of the school, and to demonstrate how it will be achieved. Human potential is important – it gives learning a sense of time and an objective. Since human potential can be developed throughout life, learning attitudes developed in school must last at least a learner's lifetime. A good lifelong learning school is aware that each individual has enormous potential and that its development is not only possible but desirable. 'Could do better' is not quite enough – it begs the question of what I, as a teacher, have to do to create the conditions under which the pupil could do better.

But the school also has a wider constituency – a difficult and diverse mixture of stakeholders in parents, governors and community members. Schools will need to carry this constituency along with them and involve them in the strategy and its purpose. Their learning needs are also of importance if the strategy is to be a coherent and a complete one. Modern businesses try to create a company culture, a sense of belonging to a worthwhile organization with worthwhile objectives and a common aim for everyone to aspire to. They do this by explaining their objectives and the strategy so that everyone, suppliers, workers, executive management, shareholders – even customers – has a sense of ownership and a set of personal goals. Schools could learn something from that. Many schools have developed an excellent school culture within their walls, but few have extended it to the outside world, for a variety of reasons:

- much of what they do – curriculum, qualification system, governing statutes – is determined by external factors;

- core objectives change little over the years;
- the burden on staff is already high;
- school administrators have little training in executive management techniques;
- fear of interference from the outside world.

Thus, schools have tended to shy away from written, and available to all, strategies. Collectively they comprise a powerful and understandable disincentive to openness. The movement to lifelong learning presents an opportunity – indeed an imperative – to schools to learn in such a way that they can reassess their *raison d'être* and their operational strategies. There are tools and techniques to enable them to prepare for their new role at the heart of the whole community – personal learning plans, learning passports, mentoring systems, skills development programmes, partnerships, new technologies, to mention just a few. These are elements of their new comprehensive strategy to develop the human potential of all those connected with school, and the means by which they progress into a lifelong learning future.

2. Involves children and staff in the maintenance of a culture of quality and respect for high standards in everything it does and in continuous improvement programmes for staff
Quality is another word widely used in industry and business. Principles of total quality management (TQM) have become the fundamental operating codes of companies around the world. The symbol of ISO9000 or BS5050 is eagerly sought since it adds to a company's credibility and hence its ability to sell its products. It works best when everyone in an organization has been immersed in quality courses; indeed that is a requirement of receiving the award. Around it are placed reward schemes at various levels, further courses in aspects of quality, information dissemination policies to inform and involve people, feedback strategies, a corporate identity, and special management policies and house styles.

Quality is also a word used in education. Few schools would confess to a lack of quality and all schools believe that the education they give is the best they can give, given the constraints of resource put upon them. But how many have suggested quality management courses for their teachers and administrative staff? And how many have thought to offer such courses for the children? And are there any schools with a suggestion box, or a grievance procedure, or a strategy for the development of quality teaching materials?

Many would argue that strategies used in industry would not work in schools. And they are right – if they are the *same* strategies. But the ideas behind them are always adaptable to new situations. A quality policy for a school, which involves the children in its formulation, is not beyond the creative capacity of educational administrators. It is an essential step towards establishing the school as a Learning Organization and, again, the resources of the community, particularly those of the industrial or business sector, can be made available to define, design and implement it.

3. Increases the resources available to the school by harnessing the skills, talents and knowledge of governors, parents, business leaders and everyone in the community to create new learning opportunities and implement school strategies

Schools are both leaders and servants of the community in which they reside. They both draw from, and contribute to, community life in many different ways and, in the final analysis, they are responsible to it as a civilizing influence. The demands upon them become ever more copious while, at the same time, the resources given to them ensure that they cannot satisfy those demands.

They are variously asked to become more open to the community and more restrictive and closed in their objectives, more flexible and more rigid, more adventurous and more timid, more gentle and more brutal, more visionary and more dogmatic. They are asked both to take on board new educational discoveries and to reject them. Small wonder that the reputation of schools has been falling. They have been given an unenviable task.

This situation will not improve without help – from national and local government to be sure in the form of more resource – above all, help from the local community which, collectively, for many schools offers an enormous, presently untapped, pool of additional knowledge, skill and talent. Many schools are ambivalent about letting parents and others into the classroom. Somehow it is seen to be an intrusion into the educational process, and sometimes it is seen to be a confession of failure on the part of teachers and the school. Indeed, the first is true – it *is* an intrusion, but a wholly positive one, in that the introduction of new knowledge, new wisdom, new outlooks widens the horizons of children and teachers. Of course it has to be effectively managed – no one would dream of giving class time to racist or political propaganda or incitement to violence. But to bring in a nurse to teach first aid, a policeman to teach safety first, a local industrialist to describe the world of work, an engineer to bolster the teaching of aspects of technology, a parent to help with reading – with creative application there are hundreds more such possibilities – can only add value and help learners learn.

Nor does it devalue the teacher. In a world in which information is doubling every five years, no one expects the teacher to have total knowledge. The teacher's most valuable function is as a trained, skilled manager.

Woodberry Down and IBM

The lifelong learning school will have many partnerships, and these will be two-way cooperation dialogues with the sole objective of improving learning in the school and in the community. One of the most fruitful partnerships is with local industry, and perhaps a case study will make the point about the possibilities which exist. It concerns a school in innercity London, Woodberry Down in the borough of Hackney, and a branch office of the multinational company IBM, situated in the City of London. Both of these locations, sadly, are gone, being the victims of company and educational reorganization, but the cooperation which was established between these two very different institutions has acted as a model for others in the UK, and is transportable to many schools throughout the world.

Schools/industry partnerships are usually established to enable teachers and children to understand the world of work and to participate in programmes which add a touch of reality to the school curriculum. Often there are extensions to this which enable teachers to attend company courses to pick up skills otherwise unavailable to them, usually connected with management.

'Twinning', as it was called, went much further than this. It recognized that at the IBM location there were 700 people, all with special skills and talents in and out of the job, and that many of these were also parents, albeit with children at very different schools. At Woodberry Down there were 1500 pupils and a staff of more than 100, comprising teachers and administrative staff. Into the middle of this was placed a half-time coordinator whose task it was to determine how each organization could enhance the operation and activities of the other. She spoke to a lot of people and established a small database of projects and people interests and talents from those willing to participate.

The activities in this four-year cooperation tell an interesting story. It should be said that this was not a commercial relationship. Both organizations were very aware of how such a programme could be misrepresented as such and IBM especially was very careful not to take commercial advantage of the twinning. Nevertheless, more than 35 events and projects, some of them recurrent annually or termly, were established. The list makes interesting reading:

- Both staff and students visited IBM to study particular areas of expertise which were of interest to them in curriculum development. There were reciprocal visits to the school by staff of IBM to give lessons on business and computing. IBM staff were invited to sit in on, and contribute to, debates in the four curriculum groups operated by the school.
- Social events included visits to each organization by the staff of the other twice per year. IBM staff had a permanent invitation to all school functions and several took advantage of this.
- A trust fund was established for voluntary contributions from staff of both organizations and the community. The money so obtained was used to create a school careers centre and send children to its Welsh study centre.
- In support of IBM's sponsorship of opera, the Covent Garden Royal Opera Company ran a workshop for children at the school. This was followed by visits to opera by the children. As a result, the school established a thriving opera club.
- Scrap computer/typewriter parts and obsolete paper stocks (including computer paper) were donated to the school.
- Contacts were established with IBM locations in Spain to assist in the school's Spanish exchange scheme.
- School staff attended IBM management courses and obtained follow-up

assistance in implementing management programmes.

- IBM staff organized a highly successful interviewing scheme for older pupils at the school. This comprised mock interviews to improve the performance of school-leavers when applying for jobs and at interview. This was an on-going programme over three years.
- Every term a debate was held, attended by the joint staffs. Topics included management by objectives, skills for a business world, social problems in innercities. They led to lively discussions between people from different backgrounds, but also did much to break down stereotypes.
- Woodberry Down children joined the IBM sail training programmes.
- IBM staff contributed to English, maths and science lessons and assisted with sports.
- Woodberry Down staff visited the IBM Educational Centre and Manufacturing Plant for enrichment of the school curriculum.

Lest one think that the flow of benefit was all one way, Woodberry Down also:

- organized a series of educational briefing sessions at IBM, which certainly improved the perceptions of IBM parents;
- allowed IBM staff the use of its sports facilities;
- assisted in a seminar given for government ministers on industry/education partnerships;
- organized frequent exhibitions of children's work at the IBM location;
- commissioned a vast collage for display in the central foyer of the IBM location, contributed to by many children in the art department, and the fee was put into the school fund.

These were projects of benefit for both organizations and excellent examples of what can be done given goodwill, genuine cooperation, a creative approach to partnerships and someone to organize the programme. Of course IBM may be an exceptional exemplar, but that is not the point. All of these and more are possible in other contexts, and not just with industry. A new marketing strategy for schools might be to involve themselves in the community and the community in themselves, in order to achieve their learning objectives and fulfil their social obligations.

4. Develops a curriculum based on the enhancement of personal skills and values to improve knowledge and understanding, and enable children to manage change throughout their lives

Much has been written on the relative intellectual paucity of the common curriculum and the irrelevance of much of it to the realities of an information-dominated world and the real needs of children for the future. Lifelong learning will not be enhanced by a content-dominated curriculum inspected only by the exercise of memory skills at a particular moment. Nevertheless, since that is the reality of present-day political domination of the schools curriculum and the reality of the way in which teachers are taught, paid and promoted, schools are in the position of having to adhere to the system.

In whatever field of endeavour, it takes a leap of both imagination and courage to break from the way things are into the way things should be and will have to be in the future. Take the issue of skills. Few skills are independent of other skills. Learning to learn, a self-evident pre-requirement for a lifelong learning society, can enhance considerably the process of memorization, the only skill which has to be demonstrated in the present system. There is no incompatibility in teaching a content-based curriculum by developing the skills which will enhance its effect, only the reluctance to change without being required or authorized to, even though common sense dictates the need. That and the unintended ignorance which stems from being under continuous pressure in the present and having no time to consider the future. At the first Global Conference on Lifelong Learning, Barrie Oxtoby of the Rover Group said, 'The development of our learning skills is probably the single most useful asset that anyone can acquire during the whole of life. How to use our senses and natural behaviours, if they are properly known to us, is of fundamental importance in the acquisition and application of new knowledge.'

Other skills are relevant to the growing child. At the same conference the major issues for schools were divided into four types of generic skills as shown below.

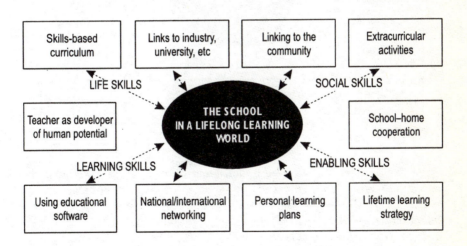

Figure 9: *Issues and skills*

The skills-based curriculum has intellectual roots going back to the early 1970s. Longworth's thesis on Information Skills in Secondary Schools Curricula contains 100 hours of course materials which practically encourage children to understand how information is all around us, how it can be analysed, acted upon, distorted, expanded and proliferated in a variety of environments. When they are properly used discovery-based methods of teaching develop attributes of curiosity, flexibility and understanding in children and are among the enabling skills which open up the mind to further explorations into learning.

But it is the life skills and the social skills which, because they are not examined, or perhaps examinable, tend to be the most neglected. These are also the skills which are most important in lifelong learning, and those for which the school is not solely responsible. They are best developed in conjunction with other partners – parents, governors, professional organizations, interest groups and industry. Figure 10 lists those which we find most attractive for the development of lifelong learning outlooks and values in children.

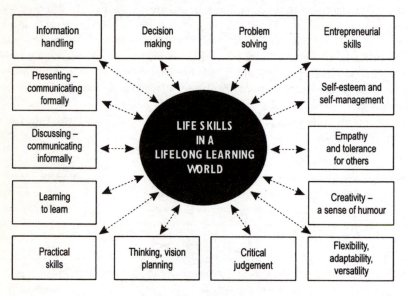

Figure 10: *Life skills in a lifelong learning world*

These skills relate to a set of educational and social ideals which tend to be unfashionable in today's utilitarian and unimaginative world, but emphasis on skills leads to greater understanding and a more receptive mind. The information ladder shown in Figure 18 (p 93) shows a progression from data to wisdom. Few people reach the top of that ladder but the lifetime of ascent represents a goal to be achieved and an interesting journey along the way. More people would get there if they were given the skills which enable them to reach the next rung at an early age.

5. Uses modern information and communications technologies wisely across all disciplines, including the exploration of collaborative learning opportunities through networks
This is an enormous topic, the subject of symposia, conferences and seminars all

over the world. Schools have been urged to come to terms with the fact of the computer in education and many have invested in computer laboratories in order to do so. And yet, in general, teachers remain unconvinced.

The key to the future lies with the development of new, exciting and interactive learning programmes which involve teachers, pupils, parents, and even members of the community in a common learning adventure.

The most exciting development in the use of technology in schools remains to be exploited. We have already described how the use of the computer as a sophisticated communications tool has the potential to bring schools into the lifelong learning age more quickly, its effect on the motivation to learn, and sometimes on the maturity of children. The following examples have already happened in some small way.

(a) 'Children interact with networks of scientists working on environmental programmes'
Many scientists are of course already in touch with each other through their own networks. However, their availability to educational networks could make them into a very valuable resource for teaching, learning and materials development, and even the teaching and learning process itself. Some experiments of involving children in such work have been carried out with NASA scientists.

(b) 'Teachers develop and teach collaboratively common curricula between schools, nationally and internationally. Children learn collaboratively with other children from different regions, countries or cultures'
Through the participation of teachers and children nationally or globally, the collaborative development and testing of courses and materials to satisfy particular requirements would be a great boon. The electronic facilities would be used for distribution of course modules, ideas for new courses, assessment of needs and much else. The increased motivation through cooperative learning is almost tangible in those places where such programmes have taken place.

(c) 'Children and teachers participate in joint project work with organizations in the community such as teacher training organizations, industrial education establishments, etc'
The opportunities for pre-service and in-service training of teachers in schools, for participation in research and development projects and for accessing the information needed to create new courses are evident. Children too can be involved in the projects.

(d) 'Children access databases nationally and internationally to develop their project work'
There are many examples of environmental databases offering access to schools. They range from the Global Monitoring Systems at UNEP-GRID, through the national ones at CORINE and NASA, to databases established by local government. All act as resources to underpin strategic teaching and learning – in which the data are made available to the learner, and it is the learner's task, assisted by the teacher, to make the right scientific inferences from the information available.

This is often a skill which is neglected in schools and so there is an allied need to incorporate into courses which use databases the mental tools and techniques which encourage careful interpretation of the resource.

(e) 'Children, helped by teachers, build up common geographical, biological, historical or other databases with children from other schools, countries or regions'
Here there is an opportunity to impart information-handling skills from the collection stage through storage, analysis and dissemination. Here also is the opportunity to recognize the value of associated high-order skills such as problem-solving, decision-making, thinking.

There are several examples. Under the PLUTO project teachers in training in Manchester, Portugal, Sweden and Belgium put together a cultural database on travel, eating and living habits using themselves as data examples. More recently, the Computer Pals around the World network engaged in a collaborative environmental data collection exercise on acid rain using 30 schools from several countries.

(f) 'Children, helped by teachers, help each other to learn languages through one to one exercises, which they create and mark themselves, using help as necessary'
The advantages of this in terms of insight, motivation and enthusiasm are evident. And the earlier this process starts the better, since young children learn languages more easily than older children and adults.

The Internet would be a useful starting point for such programmes. This is one of the best illustrations of the skills of the lifelong learning age teacher. A network in which children say hello to each other has limited value – a network in which the teacher is inserted into that communication to turn it into a living example of educational progress can provide insights which no other teaching medium can give, with the bonus of a glimpse of the real world.

6. Looks outward to the world, promoting a sense of tolerance, justice and understanding of different races, creeds and cultures in all children
These are questions of values and attitude, which schools, in partnership with other sectors of the community, are responsible for instilling in children. The best positive values tend to stem from positive self-esteem allied to humility – the realization that the road to self-discovery and the discovery of others is a long one with many pot-holes on the way, but that each one of us has the makings of an inner strength to see it through.

This means two things. First it means taking failure out of the system as far as is possible, and recognizing that short-term failure can also be a guideline for future success – both for organizations and for individuals. Organizational values therefore affect personal values. A lifelong learning school encourages the positive at all times and sets up structures and procedures which celebrate the fact of human potential and its capacity to expand.

Second, it means that the focus of the school's effort has to be on developing self-confidence, self-knowledge and self-management in each individual child. The task cannot be underestimated. Encouraging maturity is difficult, especially in the pubescent semi-adult. There are many conflicting happenings, both physical and temporal. But how many schools really put this at the forefront of their thinking, and run individual and group programmes to encourage a mature outlook? The best industrial companies run personal development programmes for all their staff. Some of the more enlightened ones take youngsters battered by their experiences of failure at an earlier age and give them the self-confidence to go forward through a renewed ability to learn. This is however a process of picking up the pieces which should not have been broken in the first place. Schools would do well to look at industry's methods in developing people – and learn from them. More than that, in a lifelong learning environment they would participate on equal terms.

7. Stimulates home–school cooperation and involves the family in the life and work of the school
The family is one of the most important units in a person's life and for most children it is a secure environment within which life can continue when everything else fails. But, as has been described in Chapter 2, in many parts of the industrial world the family communication system is breaking down and social tensions exacerbated. The generation gap tends to be wider in countries which proclaim liberty of conscience and liberty of thought. Schools are often at the difficult end of family discord. Children bring it with them into the building and demonstrate it in their behaviour.

Most schools will have their stories of the parents who won't cooperate, who abuse their children, who are the ones they should see and who never turn up for meetings with teachers. In many cases this is a result of their own bad schoolday experiences.

Nor have schools in the past been expert at communicating with the home. Thus anything that can improve this situation is a welcome advance. A lifelong learning school will try to think of strategies to make learning a family concern. It will not be easy, but achieving it will remove one of the major obstacles to the creation of a lifelong learning community. Strategies might include:

- Making the school a more community-oriented organization by devising non-threatening courses for parents, running parents' clubs and societies, encouraging sporting links between schools and parents and opening the doors to parental participation in classes, either as assistants or as learners.
- Marketing themselves better to the home. (In this they might consider consulting the publicity and marketing departments of industry.) Glossy brochures and informative handbooks and magazines with contributions from the teachers and children would give a sense of community.
- Tripartite partnership arrangements between industry, school and home. Meeting the parents in the work situation.

- Carrying out learning audits (see Chapter 4, p 66) with parents and governors. Assessing the learning needs of parents and understanding how they might be satisfied. Questionnaires might be devised by the school and personal interviews carried out by the children.
- Communicating school objectives and changes to the parents through the governors.
- Offering a parental advice service, a telephone hot-line, inviting a parental suggestion box.
- Running a brainstorming session with members of staff on ideas of how to improve home–school cooperation. Use an industry or local government friend to do this.
- Where possible, using the technology – setting homework tasks to be done on the home computer or establishing an e-mail link between school and home.
- Involving parents in extra-curricular activities – trips and journeys, school plays, sports teams, choirs, clubs and societies.
- Using friends of the school (parents, governors, members of the community who wish to make a contribution) to make friends with the school and run these programmes. They tend to be closer to the problem – and the solution.

Creative ideas are not difficult to produce and improved home–school cooperation is a prize worth seeking.

8. Expands lifelong learning in all its children and staff by involving them in the development of personal learning plans, guides and mentors

To motivate their workforce and to create the habit of learning, some industries are beginning to experiment with personal learning plans. Each person has a set of learning objectives over a period of, say, one year. They are not necessarily work-related and may include playing better tennis, wine-making or understanding opera as well as managing an assembly line, mastering a jig-tool or bringing oneself up to date with the latest in robotics. To help achieve these, a mentor – a friend, colleague or expert – may help in each topic or as an overall guide and the learner may act as a mentor to someone else. The whole ethos is non-threatening. Each plan-holder is also its owner and its author – the motivation has come from within. Qualifications may, or may not, be a part of the plan. It is an essentially simple idea but many industries have found that in raising the motivation it also raises the performance of individual people and often leads to quite dramatic improvements.

In schools there is a similar plan – it is called a timetable and a syllabus and the mentors are the teachers. But this suffers from a major drawback – the holder of the plan is not its owner, he/she has had no say in its content and its methods are imposed rather than agreed. It would not be possible to recreate the industrial model in the school environment, but the idea of ownership of one's own learning is an important one for motivation and, with a small amount of creativity, different models of the personal learning plan can be adapted for both children and teachers and remain sensitive to the needs of each individual learner. They would perhaps have to take into account factors such as motivation, background, behavioural characteristics, ability to learn quickly, preferred learning style and psychological makeup, but these too would be a step along the road to self-knowledge and, through this, self-improvement.

The burden of implementation on teachers is high, but a lifelong learning school has, as has been seen, many community resources at its disposal.

9. Broadens the vision of staff and children through a wide range of cultural experiences and extracurricular activities
Ask an adult about memories of schooldays and the answer will not reveal much about spending long hours in classrooms, examination slogs or remembering pieces of information from the curriculum. More often than not it will be about things outside the classroom – participation in the school play, songs sung in the school choir, friends made in the playground, the peculiar characteristics of certain teachers, the clubs and societies they joined, the sports teams they represented and trips organized by the school. Perhaps this gives a clue about what is of long-term importance to people and what the most educating influences were in their schooldays. Can we learn anything about how people learn from this?

Certainly the successful school has a thriving set of extracurricular activities associated with it. It also tends to be the sort of school which gains the affection of its staff and children and which retains it for a long time. Such activities also provide the opportunity for children and staff to know and respect each other through shared experiences. Participation is also learning – it is one of the most effective ways of understanding and instilling respect for any cultural field, whether it be the theatre, music, literature or sport. It goes without saying that a lifelong learning school will be one of the liveliest, most stimulating and inspiring organizations in town.

10. Celebrates learning frequently as a desirable, permanent and enjoyable habit for all.
It is not enough to keep the joy of learning to oneself. It must be celebrated and proclaimed to the community and beyond. Confident Learning Organizations will hold learning events, learning festivals, learning courses and learning parties. They will promote and publicize learning in every way. The school which can take that on board is well on the way to success as a lifelong learning institution.

Putting it together

The above principles define what a school entering the lifelong learning age of the 21st century should be aiming for. Faced with today's problems, tomorrow's opportunities may seem distant, but in order to make progress to a better, more understanding, more learning society, a start has to be made somewhere, and it is important to know the goals. A lifelong learning school is a better organization than one which does not encourage these learning values. If we do not make plans to meet the challenges of tomorrow, we continue to wallow in the problems of today.

Problems tend to have a critical mass. An attack on them now can accelerate the solution at a later date which, in turn, accelerates the solution to another problem. For example, if real home–school cooperation can be achieved, then there is the possibility of a breakthrough with the related problems of absentee-ism, antisocial behaviour and lack of motivation. These in turn can be addressed by stratagems to focus more on the needs of each learner, using help from the resources in the community.

But the key to everything is cooperation. We may not see a genuine lifelong learning community this side of the millennium but all sectors should start the process. Perhaps, taking our cue from the Cities of Learning movement, we shall also see towns, villages and regions designating themselves as learning areas. In these a lifelong learning school is seen for what it is – central to the future well-being of the community it serves, not just in educational terms but in its social and moral health too.

Schools will no longer be the Cinderellas of the system but the core of the community, adopted by partners in industry, education and local society. They will look outwards to the national and international world through electronic networks, visits, adventures and competitions. They will employ a range of professionals to help ensure the maximum development of individual human potential – teachers, assistants, medical and multimedia specialists, psychological counsellors, leaders of clubs, societies and sports, musicians, poets and authors, social scientists.

A Utopian dream? Perhaps so in today's fragmented and educationally deval-ued society, but if it can be done with a proper respect for individual differences and genuine tolerance and understanding, it is a dream worth aiming for.

Chapter 4

Learning for Earning: Learning for Survival

Lifelong learning and the workplace

Before the 1980s it would have been legitimate to ask why business and industry should be included in a book on learning. In fact, a few of the large companies, especially those in North America and Northern Europe, have always been active in promoting links with the world of education. This is partly to discharge their responsibilities to the community or nation in which they operate under the title of corporate social responsibility, and partly as a means of making up the shortfall in their own provision of education or research. The picture has expanded beyond recognition and learning is now the number one preoccupation of most industries. Many factors have influenced this change and this chapter and the next explain what these are.

The major transformation since the early 1980s is that business and industry have moved ahead of the traditional education providers in their thinking, designing and implementing of learning. While schools, colleges and universities have for the most part retained the old 'sheep and goats' perception of human potential, industry, through necessity, has been focusing on cost-effective methods of satisfying the needs of all learners. In so doing it has made some genuine breakthroughs in educational practice.

Nevertheless, the wealth-generating sectors of a nation's economy are under continuing pressure. They are variously blamed for creating unemployment, overemphasizing the profit motive, destroying the environment and being slow to react to competition. The commercial world has as much interest in survival as anyone and, like them, are daily confronted with a bewildering array of changes to which they must respond quickly in order to continue in business. Enlightened industry, whether a large multinational company, a small or medium-sized enterprise or a one-person consultancy, has to learn to cope with these changes. All types and sizes of company are neither more nor less than the sum of their human resources, and the wise organization treats that as its most precious asset.

This chapter describes how industry and business is adapting, and must adapt, by developing a learning approach to its essential operations. In rebuilding itself as a Learning Organization it is also laying the foundations of a learning society, both in the community in which it is situated and in the wider world. The successful company has to be light on its feet in order to respond to the challenges thrown up by today's complex world, ten of which are described in Figure 11.

LEARNING COMPANIES IN A LEARNING WORLD

1. Staying alive in a competitive world.
2. New work paradigms, new responses.
3. Quality programmes to stimulate learning.
4. Skills and competencies in the new economy.
5. Employment or employability.
6. Educating education – new partnerships.
7. The company and lifelong learning.
8. Accreditation is important but...
9. Broadcasting the vision and the goals.
10. New opportunities through education technology.

Figure 11: *Learning companies in a learning world*

1. Staying alive in a competitive world

'The need for a learning society to convert and compete is not just urgent. It is a matter of economic life and death. It is a matter of social success or disaster. It is a matter of survival.' (Cann in Bradshaw, 1995)

Industrial competition is fiercer now than at any time in history. The industrial-ized world has expanded considerably and the 'tiger economies' of the Pacific Rim are rapidly catching up, and in some cases overtaking, the traditional industrial nations of Japan, Europe and North America. While there is expanding world-wide demand this represents a challenge, but not necessarily a survival threat, to these countries. However, in times of world slump, an over-capacity of manu-facturing capability can send the unprepared and the under-resourced to the wall. Even in times of economic health and growth, the pressures of competition are hardly more comfortable. Modern businesses have to plan their strategies on the assumption of a constantly changing short-term and an increasingly unknown long term.

Add to this the (usually justified) concerns of environmentalists to promote sustainable development of the earth's resources, the intense pressure to use technology in an attempt to become more efficient, the necessity for working partnerships with schools, universities, other companies, suppliers and custom-ers, the constant need to update and improve products in order to remain competitive, and one begins to understand the managerial nightmare faced by modern industry. The traditional top-down management and authoritarian working methods can no longer cope with the diversity and complexity of modern production demands. The industrial society paradigm of hierarchical management control from the executive suite, every worker in his place and a slowly changing production line is obsolete – it simply cannot cope with the real world. A new set of strategies is taking over, based on the empowerment of the workforce. Decision-making has moved down the line and created the need for well thought out decisions from an understanding of the basic need for efficiency and knowledge by people who have not traditionally had that responsibility in the past. It is a world of trust in the capability of people, backed by continuous education and updating, to make effective decisions.

The effect of this empowerment means constant education and training of the whole workforce, not just in tools, techniques and methods but also in the wider aspects of business, management and international competition. The new survival imperative for companies which wish to survive is to invest in learning – to become a Learning, as well as a production, Organization. This is as true in the service industries as it is in the primary and secondary sectors of industry.

2. New work paradigms, new responses

'Much unemployment is structural, arising from a growing gap between the need to adapt to change, and the economy's and society's ability and even willingness to change. The solution lies in a thorough examination and reform of all the policies which bear on the capacity and willingness to adapt and to innovate in the face of technological change and intensifying global competition.' (OECD, 1996)

Mass production techniques using the Tayloristic model of intense, robot-like functional specialization is no longer a viable option. For one thing, the robots do this much better, and for another, the customer demands flexibility and the tailoring of product. The new theme-song is tailor, rather than Taylor, and this is much more in tune with the new global, rapidly changing, networked world.

In the past, organizations have been tied to economies of scale, successful through their ability to produce high volumes of standardized goods and services at low prices. However, today's customers are more sophisticated. They require a choice, a custom-made product, high quality with zero defects and a short time scale for delivery. Today's marketplace thrives on new products with high levels of creativity and innovation and, above all, the ability to react rapidly to new applications based on new ideas. When the lifespan of products has become shorter there is a need for rapid adaptation and for the workforce to learn new things faster. Companies cannot spend two years learning new techniques if the new technologies on which they are based need to be marketed in nine-month cycles. Further, if speed of response is an important success factor, accuracy of timing is even more important. Hence the recent innovation of just-in-time production, based on the right mixture of production and product development, marketing, logistics and satisfying the needs of the customer, a procedure implemented to meet this challenge.

This new requirement of improved productivity creates the need to employ people who can add value and eliminate waste. In production terms, a competitive company is one which can concentrate its efforts on an accurate selection of key areas of activity and an appropriate adjustment to these economies of scope.

3. Quality programmes to stimulate learning

'In the past decade, efforts concentrated on rationalization and automation in order to increase productivity, an important determinant of unit labour costs and thus price competitiveness. The strategic means to achieve this was investment in fixed capital. To be more productive and competitive in the 1990s will call for a greater emphasis on improving quality and innovation through investment in education and training for skills.' (European Commission, *Guidelines for Community Action* 1993)

For some time quality has been the driving force behind the activities of most modern companies. The quality movement has firmly established itself as a major agent of change for the better. Those of us who can remember the times spent at the roadside, often in the rain, repairing a car which had broken down for inexplicable reasons, know that the frequency of this happening has diminished tenfold and more. All our household appliances, too, function more or less without need of repair for long periods of time.

The education function has not been exempt. Companies are now far better at forecasting and satisfying the training needs of many of their employees, and in many instances have progressed further into concepts of continuous improvement. The continuing development of the competence of employees has to be the main focus of a modern, lean organization. The adaptability, skill and commitment of its workforce is the key strategic asset of any organization because it both creates and sustains the ability of the organization to compete and thrive. This involves a much more integrated approach. An organization providing just-in-time service to customers must have all its operations, including learning and the improved competence of the workforce, well coordinated.

4. Skills and competencies in the new economy

'Individuality, creativity, the ability to think for oneself – the values we treasure in modern industry – were (in the industrial society) hardly considered to be assets on the assembly line, or even in the executive suite.' (Naisbitt and Aburdine, 1986)

Treating the worker as a resource can have a dehumanizing effect. An industrial robot is also a resource in that sense. Even the repackaging of the old personnel department into the more comprehensive 'Department of Human Resources' gives a sign that the employee is still perhaps a cog in the company machine, rather than a human being with a wider range of life objectives of which the company is just one. This is a reasonable attitude and a superficially true statement of the reality from the company point of view. However, new perceptions are at work.

New, more holistically oriented theories propose that a more integrated approach to an individual's *total* learning needs would increase commitment and improve performance. They recommend the adoption of strategies to develop the full human potential of employees, and, because of this, their learning needs have to be looked at as a whole. As one American Director of Human Resources has said, 'I no longer have a Human Resources strategy – I have 2000 human resource strategies. One for each employee.' In this environment, learning replaces the word 'training', the former being an activity for human beings, the latter an activity more suitable for robots.

New working methods, based on competencies and speed, need highly competent, multiskilled experts with a broad set of skills and competencies and who are entrepreneurs, not machines. Further, the urgency for greater effectiveness in the marketplace requires that all employees become more aware of a company's objectives, and that they strive towards jointly defined goals with the higher order mental tools and means to achieve them.

Nor is this a one-time requirement. Individuals, whatever their specific fields, must cope with business demands that require them to renew their knowledge and competence continuously. In many instances professional education must be completely renewed three or four times during a person's career, or a professional person may have several completely new careers during a lifetime. There is a lifelong need for upgrading, updating and relearning. This is especially acute in the fields of engineering and technology, where the rapid pace of development creates new applications almost weekly.

Figure 12 summarizes the new skills. It highlights how the old skills based on memory and manual competence are being replaced by knowledge and brain skills requiring mental dexterity and problem-solving capability. Factual knowledge and hard skills are only a small part of the learning requirement. Experience gained in all areas of life is also valuable. This shift from a focus on training and teaching to a focus on learning on the part of the workforce imposes a new approach to learning and new structures to enable it on the part of both the company and the individual. The stimulation of the habit of learning becomes a paramount consideration, and many companies offer financial inducements to their employees to take courses, whether or not these are connected with the business.

With many honourable exceptions, current employer-based training often lacks this wider vision. It provides programmes to develop job-based competencies in people, but it sometimes lacks the essential insights for understanding personal and corporate needs for the future. The development of a longer-term outlook is not easily taught by traditional means. It involves personal values, mature attitudes and a confident self-knowledge from each individual, rather than facts, skills or competencies and, because of this, it demands a greater focus on the learner and the means of learning.

SKILLS FOR A LIFELONG LEARNING AGE

Learning to learn	Knowing one's learning style Being able to 'pile up' knowledge and to combine new information with the existing
Putting new knowledge into practice	Seeing the connection between theory and practice Transferring knowledge from the head to the hands
Questioning and reasoning	Being continuously aware of changes Curiosity Assessing information
Managing oneself and others	Setting realistic targets and communicating them to others Recognizing the gap between the current and the target and understanding how to fill the gap
Managing information	Retrieving, analysing and combining information Using information technology
Communication skills	Ability to express oneself verbally and in writing
Team work	Sharing information Receiving information Collaborating Achieving goals
Problem-solving skills	Creativity and innovation
Adaptability and flexibility	Facing changes Adapting to new situations and tasks
Understanding the responsibility of updating and upgrading one's own competence	Understanding competence development needs and the value of competence Developing one's competence

Figure 12: *Skills for a lifelong learning age.*
(Adapted from WILL, Community Action for Lifelong Learning, 1995)

5. Employment or employability

'The concept of work is continuously changing. An individual not only has several jobs in a lifetime, but may also have several careers. Therefore, everybody needs continuous updating and upgrading of skills and competence throughout working life.' (ERT, 1989)

The concept of lifetime employment is vanishing at the same speed as businesses and industries restructure. The multinationals, which have a tradition of training, retraining and promoting from within, and in so doing have created great loyalties to the company culture and ethic, are rapidly down- (or right-) sizing. Even the large Japanese companies are being forced to re-examine this, one of the most sacred of their practices. Such are the numbers involved – IBM in the UK reduced from 18,000 to 12,000 from 1990 to 1995 and is widely tipped to shed more jobs – that the process of acquiring and maintaining a job in the future will be very different. No longer will the universities be trawled for talent in the annual 'milk round', no longer will several thousands of graduates be taken into the bosom of the great companies for the remainder of their working lives. Instead, large enterprises will employ a highly educated, highly paid, highly productive core staff to run the core business and out-source all their other requirements to specialist providers.

This core staff will need to be innovative, adaptable and highly educated in order to maintain the company's competitive advantage, as will the coterie of companies on which they will now rely for specialist services. All will need to be quick on their feet, quick to learn new requirements and cultures, able to demonstrate relevance to a company's needs and employ people who are adaptable, flexible and versatile. Some of them will be very small organizations employing two or three people, but all are lifelong learning organizations employing lifelong learners. Indeed lifelong learning is the *sine qua non* of the new employability.

Companies can go only so far in providing learning opportunities. They can stimulate, recommend and provide, but the essential motivation to take advantage of what is offered must come from the individuals themselves. The more that people invest in up-to-date education, the more they are investing in personal opportunities for advancement and promotion. In today's climate staying in employment means staying employable, and that means developing the ability to gain new knowledge quickly and to adapt to the needs of the marketplace.

Such is the need for adaptability and a wide appreciation of the needs of the job that some companies are working without detailed or explicit job descriptions. An example of this is the Rover Group, which has completely revised its methods of working. The case study in Chapter 5 (pages 79–84) describes how employees are 'empowered', given the skills and knowledge which enable them to make decisions and solve problems, and capable and willing to do the work that is available and needed at any time. In this environment each person needs to be kept up to date with the use of the new technologies and to understand how they can improve performance and throughput.

Such a continuous process of adaptation to the needs of the workplace demands flexibility by both organizations and individuals. It can only be sustained through the adoption of individual attitudes which accept continuous learning as a fact of life and organizational attitudes which encourage and motivate such learning. Hence the movement in many companies towards the creation of Learning Organizations. For the individual, learning is employability and employability is learning. For the organization, learning is survival and survival is learning. For both, lifelong learning is lifelong earning.

6. Educating education – new partnerships

'Dialogue between industry and higher education needs to be maintained and strengthened, working towards new modes of partnership with clear goals and actions. If higher education–industry collaboration is to thrive, it must be based on clear understanding of the nature of higher education and business. Aims and objectives are best shared when the partners respect the differences in the primary functions of business and higher education'. (Commission of the European Communities, 1992)

Learning Organizations cannot exist in a self-contained educational vacuum. They draw their workforce from schools, universities and colleges which have very different cultures, values and objectives, both from the company workplace and between each other. It is the task of the organization to create a set of positive and worthwhile company values from this human raw material and to encourage the habit of learning in each one. How much easier this would be if there were a learning society in the wider world which encouraged these virtues. In its absence, however, companies must employ their own internal strategies to cope.

There is also much that the enlightened company can do to help create learning opportunities outside of the company environment. Companies have two sorts of need from the formal education system. First, they use it to give their employees, especially their scientists and technical staff, a continuing education to keep them updated and innovative. This is even more necessary where companies have downsized and out-sourced large parts of their education and training function. Issues of continuing education are dealt with in Chapter 7, but the key obligation is to create a two-way partnership with the organization delivering the continuing education. At a pre-competitive level some companies are sharing basic training and retraining opportunities and many are looking to universities and other educational institutions to assist them.

However, continuing education is only a small part of lifelong learning. If companies want to increase the likelihood that the skills, values and attitudes which they need in order to function are properly developed, they need to make an appropriate contribution to the education system outside of the company. This is the second type of two-way partnership. It encourages relationships with schools, universities and colleges, and constitutes one of the ways by which business and industry contribute to the development and maintenance of a learning society in the community in which it operates.

Partnerships with schools are of especial interest. The essence of such partnerships is a two-way process of communication in which both companies and schools can articulate and debate their respective roles, and contribute to each other's thinking. In this way stereotypes are cast aside and genuine, non-threatening cooperation takes place. The issue of schools–industry partnerships has been discussed in detail in Chapter 3. Twinning, the case study discussed on pp 46–8, has produced a great deal of interest among employers, largely because of the imaginative projects which resulted from such a close relationship.

There is increasingly a third need, and this concerns the provision of a vast number and range of courses in colleges and adult education institutes to enable employees to develop the learning habit. This type of two-way partnership between company and education system is essential in the new working environment and could be enhanced and better understood through the use of learning audits (see section 7 below).

Lifelong learning is a major challenge for educational institutions. Students from business and industry give universities access to front-line development and real-life experience. They can also provide additional financial resources to educational institutions to compensate for the cutting of public budgets.

North America has a very strong tradition of companies contributing to schools and universities, with billions of dollars targeted in this direction. While some may ask what the return on that investment has been, others are describing what the situation in both industry and society would have been like if it had not been made. In Europe, too, there are excellent examples of innovative partnership programmes with both schools and universities. The Rover Group in the UK has encouraged the production of over 1000 postgraduates in the past five years, Nokia in Finland has stimulated hundreds of PhD, MSc, and BSc degrees in engineering in the past six years and ABB, Sweden, has for numerous years offered engineers with college degrees (BSc Eng) the opportunity to continue studies towards university degrees (MSc Eng) by organizing more than half of the studies needed. However, where the administration of universities is strongly centralized, as in some of the southern European countries, the two-way cooperative process does not seem to work well.

7. The company and lifelong learning

'There is a particular challenge for manufacturing and service industries and business. It is to recognize and act upon the strong relationship between learning, investment and profit. Large and small firms alike should entrust the role of "champion of company learning" to a named main board director to provide leadership, while ensuring that the learning culture is embedded throughout the company.' (Ball and Stewart, 1995).

Good companies and employers look after the employability, as well as the employment, of their workforce. They provide employees with information about future job requirements and competence needs, encourage people to pursue learning outside of work and organize opportunities to study by bringing universities and educational institutions to the workplace. They support studies financially and reward educational achievements, and can also provide study counselling and assist individuals in making personal lifelong learning plans.

But how do companies obtain the information about the learning needs and demands of so many and different people? One answer lies in the 'learning audit' – basically a questionnaire and a means of analysing its results. The learning audit was developed in ELLI with a grant from the Force Programme of the European Commission. In principle, it takes into account a wide range of learning needs from the point of view of an individual employee rather than from that of the company. In this way a database of learning requirements can be made and discussed with a range of local learning providers. Naturally the company is not expected to satisfy all these requirements.

The learning audit is best carried out in partnership with a university or another type of education provider – that way employees have more confidence in the confidentiality of their responses. This is important because the question-naire asks for data about their past, present and future learning experiences and requirements and for opinions as well as facts. In other words, it tries to involve the individual in a detailed personal discussion about the world as he or she sees it and the place of learning in it. The range of questions is wide, as shown below.

THE RANGE OF THE LEARNING AUDIT

Past:
- Personal experience
- Personal qualifications
- Financial support given
- Opinions on past education
- In and out of company education
- Community involvement

Present:
- Personal self-assessment (strengths)
- Personal opinions of current job
- Personal ambitions
- Why should/do I learn?
- What should I learn?
- Opinions on learning

Future:
- Personal expectations
- Personal opinion on future world
- Future personal needs for learning
- Who is responsible for paying, for providing?
- Future needs for sons/daughters
- Qualifications necessary?
- Learning counsellors useful?
- In and out of company education
- Subjects wanted to learn
- Skills to be acquired

Figure 13: *The range of the learning audit*

There are questions about personal learning styles and preferences, observations on the company and its performance in satisfying their needs, enquiries about their own view of themselves, and discussions on dreams for their children. It is a complete document, opening up the mind of interviewee and interviewer alike, and supplying more information about the individual than most surveys of this type. Personal interview is recommended, though this may be impractical in locations with a large number of employees.

Learning audits may not yet be in common use, but the company of the future will make use of them both as a motivator of learning and as a means of obtaining a full picture of learning needs. The results obtained in Europe were interesting. The major difference in perception occurred between northern and southern Europe. The concept of lifelong learning as a whole-of-life activity, in which life at work and life outside of work are part of the same continuum is more resisted in southern Europe, where the lines of demarcation seem to be more rigidly applied by both individuals and companies. Similarly, the burden of deciding who takes education and when is more a matter for the individual in northern Europe than in the south.

These seemed to affect workforce perceptions on the likelihood of education and training being made available easily and freely to individuals. In all parts of the survey, even where the company provided schemes and cash for the individual employee to enjoy learning, there was some scepticism, reflecting on the one hand a failure in the company information and communication system and on the other a lack of insight into the true nature of lifelong learning. There is a long way to go before the concept of developing one's own human potential through learning, or even that one has a greater potential, is well accepted. Formal education systems seem to have done a good job in hiding it from the vast majority of people. And yet raising consciousness of its existence is important for the future of business and industry.

8. Accreditation is important, but…

'It is no longer sufficient to learn and qualify in the early part of a career and then seek to make a living out of that process for a further 40 or 50 years.' (John Hillier in Bradshaw, 1995)

The audit also confirmed one or two other thoughts. Recognition and reward act as great motivators for learning, and most people want some acknowledgment of their personal investment in learning. This operates at several levels. Many companies offer financial inducements to learn and many offer rewards on the completion of successful learning. Credits, diplomas, and degrees can serve both as a sign of a personal achievement and as evidence that a milestone has been reached in the progress of lifelong learning. At present, the award at national level of credits for studies is normally the responsibility of universities and other national accreditation organizations, although in some countries much work is being done on the harmonization of the recognition of learning, wherever it takes place. Much of it is through modularization, in which company-based courses qualify for credits along with courses being offered elsewhere, the result being a national qualification. The knowledgeable participation of companies in this process is crucial to the success of such a scheme, and it involves further partnership with universities and others.

There are, however, other levels at which the recognition of accreditation is important. Today's increasingly global working world means a much greater movement of people across international boundaries. The recognition of another country's qualifications is a minefield. Each one seems to claim superiority over the other, each has a different time scale for achieving the same apparent level, each has a different content and methodology and each is irrevocably wedded to its own system. It seems unlikely that any country is going to change its system quickly enough to cope with the march of international work requirements.

Perhaps the need is for a supra-national body to work out a system of equivalencies of qualification and to produce an international register which harmonizes the recognition of qualifications. Even then, many countries might find ways of ignoring this. Some progress has been made in Finland on the concept of a 'learning passport', which describes the holder's education, skills, competencies and qualifications. This allows lifelong learners to transport their knowledge and skills from region to region and country to country and acts as a guarantee of the achievement of a level of learning which industry could use.

These concepts are well accepted in those countries where education is a key part of the industrial and national culture, for example in South Korea where 80% of people continue their studies beyond high school, and where the acquisition of a series of qualifications is a part of the move towards a national lifelong learning society. In others, particularly in parts of Europe and North America, such a culture is, as yet, undeveloped.

University-controlled examination and assessment systems usually deal with the younger age groups, but there is also a need for such systems to be tailored to adults. These would include mechanisms for crediting non-formal learning and in-company education programmes. The UK has started this process with its NVQ (National Vocational Qualification) and GNVQ systems but it will be some time before such an approach catches the international imagination.

This somewhat academic discussion on qualifications may seem to be a long way from the interests of business and industry. But is this so? Industry has to be interested in the motivation of its workforce for its own survival. Industry also spends a great deal of its time picking up the pieces of national failure-oriented education systems. Neither workforce empowerment nor lifelong learning are about competition between individuals in industry – rather they rely on teamwork – a cooperative solution to everyday problems. This is not only true of companies, but of government departments, educational institutions and everywhere the new work ethic impinges. All these organizations need to contribute to the debate on qualification and accreditation systems and so avoid the present bitter experience of coping with its results.

9. Broadcasting the vision and the goals

Good companies invest in the development of the human potential of all their employees rather than in education and training programmes. This entails a whole person approach to learning and is the first step towards the development of a true Learning Organization within the company and a learning society outside. Since a learning society is a stable society, companies have an interest in developing and maintaining that in which they operate best.

This is one aspect of the vision which companies will need to develop in order to survive. Another is the aim of being the best. 'World class' is a term commonly used by today's Learning Organizations. The business plan of every company has to include strategies to keep three constituencies happy – customers, employees and shareholders. While there may be some small conflict between their interests, it is possible to reconcile these and to unite them into a team through an effective communications strategy.

A lifelong learning company articulates its vision to everyone, in terms which everyone can understand and relate to. The vision permeates the management system, the education and training system, and a company's relations with all the other organizations with which it does business. The effective communication of the company vision leads to effective quality and continuous improvement strategies, achievable company and departmental objectives and the easier introduction and acceptance of plans and programmes to maintain competitiveness. These may include personal learning plans for each member of the workforce and a system of mentors and guides to help them develop and succeed.

The issue of empowerment has to be faced. It involves communicating to everyone what needs to be done, what needs to be known, what needs to learned and why all these are important. It then involves a trust in the capacity of people to respond to that challenge. Empowerment is a major leadership function today.

Managers now become mentors, whose most important task is to help individuals organize their learning and to provide learning opportunities. Since learning plans are now a part of all business processes, manager/mentor is a crucial supporting function in the achievement of business objectives. Coaching and mentoring have proved to be hugely successful in the Japanese business environment, and they have been successfully modified and introduced in many Japanese companies operating in other countries.

10. New opportunities through education technology

'In a society based far more on the production, transfer and sharing of knowledge than on trade in goods, access to theoretical and practical knowledge must necessarily play a major role. As 80% of the European labour force of the year

2000 is already now in the labour market, all measures must be based on developing systematic lifelong learning and continuing training. This will involve more flexible and more open systems of training, including the use of new decentralized multimedia tools.' (Telematics for Flexible and Distance Learning – Final Report of the European Union DELTA Programme).

Lifelong learning increases a company's educational requirements by a considerable margin. The majority of the future requirement will be for people who are unaccustomed to a continuous regime of formal learning and who may have difficulty in adjusting. However, for understandable reasons, companies will be unwilling to increase their educational budgets in order to cope. Other providers of learning and other means of providing it have to be found. This means the copious use of education technology tools and techniques including distance learning, multimedia open learning methods with CD-ROM, DVI and software using multilevel, multidirectional, hypermedia approaches with combinations of text, sound, video and graphics. It also means partnerships with other education providers, both to teach in traditional classroom mode and to devise the technology-based programmes. Perhaps most importantly it means potential cost effectiveness, the ability to get through to more people, more effectively and therefore at less cost.

Some solutions already exist for a variety of people, including scientists, engineers and executive management, to keep themselves updated in their own fields of specialization. For some time now USA multinationals have been using interactive electronic classrooms for in-company tutored video instruction from a central point. These are also used for receiving broadcasts from universities so that employees can follow degree and non-degree courses via satellite. The National Technological University is a case in point. Established in the mid-1980s by several of the largest multinational companies, it has continued to broadcast courses by satellite from major American universities to industry in order to keep engineers and scientists up to date in their own fields and to enable them to obtain masters degrees while at work. It even has its degree awarding ceremonies by satellite.

The European equivalent was EuroPACE (European Programme for Advanced Continuing Education). Its demise is a reflection of the high cost of European satellite broadcasting compared with North America, the fragmented nature of European university education (in some countries engineers study to masters degree level while at university) and, regrettably, of European attitudes to investment in Continuing Education. EuroPACE 2 now operates as an interuniversity broadcasting system from the Katholieke Universiteit Leuven in Belgium.

Many companies optimize the use of their computers by using them both to receive new information about courses, processes, techniques and opportunities and to give access to screen-based education programs for employees. However, the development cost of these is often high, and companies are increasingly combining to share the development of pre-competitive open learning software. Many small companies have been established in most major industrial countries to satisfy this burgeoning demand.

Summary

How do we summarize the importance of lifelong learning to business and industry? In our view, it is not just a matter of getting it right, it is a matter of life and death for a company. Learning can be an expensive business, but the price of ignorance can be much greater. John Dewey, the educational philosopher, defined learning as 'the continual process of discovering insights, inventing new possibilities for action, and observing the consequences leading to new insights'. This a fair definition of what the Rover Group is trying to create in the whole of its workforce, and what it has empowered it to do (see Chapter 5). It is also what many of the large American multinationals and the companies in the Pacific Rim countries are doing. And it is why most of these companies are in a position to respond quickly to changes in technology, changes in customer fashion and changes in world trade patterns.

Nor do they do this by themselves. They use the resources of the educational and government systems around them, at the same time contributing to their development and progress. They are helping to create, and play their part in, an iterative learning feedback system which we may ultimately call a 'Learning society'. This can be local at the community level, national at the country level or global, where the company has a global influence. They treat their employees as learning citizens of this wider learning society, and they empower them – not through any blind faith conviction that empowered workers automatically make the right decisions, but through giving them the learning to understand company and customer needs, and ownership of the solution to those needs. 'Giving them the learning' means also stimulating people to want to learn, to making it rewarding and where possible to making it fun. It is a part of the new 'stakeholder society'.

Perhaps to their own surprise, companies are the new leaders in education. They employ modern learning techniques, manage education properly, deliver it assiduously and with invited feedback, and in general make up for the deficiencies of underfunded public systems in the schools, colleges and universities. Lifelong learning is also about sharing that leadership, putting governments right about priorities and eventually putting educational leadership back in the hands of the professionals on a whole community basis. Out-sourcing accelerates that process into a necessity. It will be some considerable time before the dawn of enlightenment, because lifelong learning is an ongoing process which has only just begun. If we do not make progress quickly, however, the discontinuities will become more marked and the bridges more difficult to cross.

Chapter 5

Turning to Learning: The Growth of Learning Organizations

The learner in the service of the organization

The movement to Learning Organizations, initiated in business and industry in the early 1980s, is now gathering pace. Multinational companies have been faced with three challenges.

1. The task of constantly retraining and redeploying their workforces in response to changing technology and new working requirements became very expensive.
2. The need to respond quickly to the competitive marketplace and shorter product lead times meant that hierarchical management structures were no longer efficient or effective.
3. The new corporate imperative to downsize and keep a core staff, bringing in expertise as required, demanded a much higher level of education and operation in existing staff and suppliers.

The response to all three was the urgent need to develop, and satisfy, the learning habit in all their employees. Smaller companies found themselves in a similar position and have followed suit in order to compete. Effectively, all these companies, multinational, small and medium enterprises (SMEs) alike, became Learning Organizations. But what exactly is meant by the term 'Learning Organization' and why has it assumed messianic proportions in recent years?

Here are two definitions. First the systems viewpoint as expressed by Michael Marquardt at the First Global Conference on Lifelong Learning.

> 'A Learning Organization is systematic, accelerated learning that is accomplished by the organizational system as a whole rather than the learning of individual members within the system. Learning Organizations are able to transform data into value knowledge and thereby increase the long-term adaptive capacity.'

The second has a slightly different, but entirely consistent, focus and was written by Jack Horgan, Director of Eurotecnet, as a foreword to *The Learning Organization: A Vision for Human Resource Development* (Stahl, et al., 1993).

> 'A Learning Organization is one which has a vision of tomorrow, seeing the people who make up the organization not simply being trained and developed to meet the organization's ends in a limiting and prescriptive manner, but for a more expanded role. Once an organization accepts that it wishes to enable or empower its personnel, the important issue which emerges is whether this empowering process is to be limited or to be permitted to drive the organization. To curtail or limit the process cannot be said to be empowerment but simply permitted change and adaptation. Empowerment raises crucial issues concerning leadership, decision-making, and the ownership of activities and their results. It is these issues which lie at the heart of the Learning Organization.'

So Learning Organizations are mostly about the empowerment of the workforce and, through this, the need for a complete reorientation of a company's total strategy towards learning as a means of doing this. This goes right to the heart of the issue, as the issue of empowerment presents great difficulties for traditional management structures and, because of this, is a nettle which many companies find hard to grasp.

A Learning Organization is also variously described as a customer orientation and quality driven culture; or team-based organization; or the provision of learning opportunities and learning tools where and when required; or coaching, mentoring, and management involvement, with lifelong learners as the strategic resource. Business gain may be the main reason to become a Learning Organization; but the means to achieve those gains is through the development of the human potential in the workforce.

All of these definitions may give the impression that the concept of a Learning Organization is only relevant to industry. Nothing could be further from the truth. Because the focus is on the needs of the customer other organizations could, and should, be examining how they can best serve their clientele. These include universities, national and local government departments, schools, teacher training organizations, professional bodies, hospitals, organizations big and small. They are all embryo Learning Organizations and each would benefit from a new approach to the way in which they look outwards to the world, if indeed they do look out at all. The journey towards becoming a true Learning Organization involves difficult decisions and some real operating adjustments.

Let us examine the characteristics of a Learning Organization in more detail. Figure 14 gives ten first characteristics, but the essence of true Learning Organizations is that they change because they learn about themselves. The learning is an iterative and continuous process, and therefore the Learning Organization, paradoxically, can never become an organization which can be said to have learned. There is always more learning to be done.

TEN CHARACTERISTICS OF A LEARNING ORGANIZATION

1. A Learning Organization can be a company, a professional association, a university, a school, a city, a nation or any group of people, large or small, with a need and a desire to improve performance through learning.
2. A Learning Organization invests in its own future through the education and training of all its people.
3. A Learning Organization creates opportunities for, and encourages, all its people in all its functions to fulfil their human potential:
   - as employees, members, professionals or students of the organization
   - as ambassadors of the organization to its customers, clients, audiences and suppliers
   - as citizens of the wider society in which the organization exists
   - as human beings with the need to realize their own capabilities.
4. A Learning Organization shares its vision of tomorrow with its people and stimulates them to challenge it, to change it and to contribute to it.
5. A Learning Organization integrates work and learning and inspires all its people to seek quality, excellence and continuous improvement in both.
6. A Learning Organization mobilizes all its human talent by putting the emphasis on 'learning' and planning its education and training activities accordingly.
7. A Learning Organization empowers *all* its people to broaden their horizons in harmony with their own preferred learning styles.
8. A Learning Organization applies up to date open and distance delivery technologies appropriately to create broader and more varied learning opportunities.
9. A Learning Organization responds proactively to the wider needs of the environment and the society in which it operates, and encourages its people to do likewise.
10. A Learning Organization learns and relearns constantly in order to remain innovative, inventive, invigorating and in business.

Figure 14: *Ten characteristics of the learning organization*

1. A Learning Organization can be a company, a professional association, a university, a school, a city, a nation or any group of people, large or small, with a need and a desire to improve performance through learning
This sets the parameters for Learning Organizations. Nothing is excluded and the only requirement is to stimulate and kindle the desire to learn in all members of the grouping. This extends to cities, towns, regions and nations as Learning Organizations within a learning society.

2. A Learning Organization invests in its own future through the education and training of all its people
The emphasis here is on the two words 'invests' and 'all'. There should be a clear

link between the development of an organization's human resource and its economic and/or operational future. Learning is an investment for the future in every sense – in future credibility, in future integrity, in future honour, in future satisfaction, in future contentment, in future stability, in future legitimacy in society, in future profit, in future viability, in future survival. To ensure this, the learning culture should be available to everyone in the organization from the woman at the top to the man who sweeps the floors. Further, everyone should not just be invited to join it, not even just encouraged, but inspired and stimulated, and rewarded for doing so.

3. A Learning Organization creates opportunities for, and encourages, all its people in all its functions to fulfil their human potential:

- as employees, members, professionals or students of the organization
- as ambassadors of the organization to its customers, clients, audiences and suppliers
- as citizens of the wider society in which the organization exists
- as human beings with the need to realize their own capabilities

The next step is make the opportunities for learning available to all. As Shakespeare said, 'Each man in his time plays many parts' and, in the modern day, the roles listed above are those which everybody plays for most of their life. Learning permeates every one of these, though the nature of that learning may change dependent on which role is being adopted. This characteristic widens the role of the organization from one which educates and trains its people for the job to one which can make itself responsible, if the learner so wishes, for the complete range of learning needs of everyone who works for it. This would include strategies for stimulating the habit of learning and for satisfying the developed habit. It need not necessarily encompass responsibility for paying for all the courses which every employee wishes to take, but it may include financial incentives to take courses and rewards.

4. A Learning Organization shares its vision of tomorrow with its people and stimulates them to challenge it, to change it and to contribute to it
This is challenging. It implies that every employee has a right to know what the company's vision is and the right to a say in the way in which the vision develops. More than that, the organization encourages employees to exercise that right. The first is easily communicated but, for a variety of reasons, very few organizations implement the second part of this radical transformation. Nevertheless, good leaders know that a sense of responsibility for the direction which an organization is taking can be a powerful motivator, and it will certainly stimulate the desire to learn accordingly.

5. A Learning Organization integrates work and learning and inspires all its people to seek quality, excellence and continuous improvement in both

This characteristic advocates quality – an essential for modern day business, but not practised in formal terms in other types of organization. When work and learning share essentially the same objectives, that of making sure that the best potential is developed from both, and all employees are empowered to reach those objectives, the organization will profit from that synergy. In an empowered work environment problems are solved and decisions are made at the workplace rather than in the classroom. Thus the workplace becomes also the 'learnplace' and the means by which this can be effected may include the provision of books and manuals, computer aided learning, audiovisual aids, access to databases etc at the point of decision-making. In this new environment managers become educators and trainers, stimulators of learning rather than controllers and prescribers.

6. A Learning Organization mobilizes all its human talent by putting the emphasis on 'learning' and planning its education and training activities accordingly

This moves education forward from the process of teaching and training to that of learning. The focus is on the needs and demands of each individual learner, and the delivery of education adapts to that new paradigm. This is the essence of lifelong learning and distinguishes it from the old method of imposing large quantities of information onto people and hoping that some of it sticks. In addition the increased confidence the learner obtains from this approach will tend to unlock a creative potential which can only be of great benefit to the organization. The new emphasis is on the acquisition of a completely different set of skills and attributes, similar to those described in Chapters 3 and 6 for children and teachers. The high order skills of information-handling, problem-solving, thinking, cooperating, communicating, insight and intuition, self-esteem and self-knowledge described in Figure 10 (p 50) become more important and more valuable. They are skills more easily digested through personal strategies for learning, rather than taught skills obtained through the traditional education and training approach.

7. A Learning Organization empowers all its people to broaden their horizons in harmony with their own preferred learning styles

People have different ways of learning. Some would prefer traditional classroom education in front of a teacher so that they can ask questions if they are stuck. Others, perhaps a majority, do not like to make their lack of knowledge public in front of their peer group and prefer to ask questions in a different way. Some would like a sit-with-Nellie approach, learning from an expert on the job. Yet others, especially those with remedial problems, may prefer to learn by computer, where no human value judgements are being made about their progress and performance.

Learning choice is learning empowerment. It enables people to move at their own speed and in their own way. Learning Organizations bear this in mind and satisfy it as far as possible. Qualifications also play a part for many, but they should be presented as a series of non-threatening challenges to each learner to improve individual performance rather than a competitive examination which highlights failure.

8. A Learning Organization applies up to date open and distance delivery technologies
appropriately to create broader and more varied learning opportunities
We have already mentioned the many ways in which education can be delivered both locally and from external sources. The use of modern education technology tools and techniques makes good financial sense. For example, broadcasts by satellite for high level engineers from centres of expertise is a cost-effective way of keeping them up to date, since they do not have to leave the workplace to receive them. Open Learning courses using multimedia presentation techniques can be made available to a higher number of students than can be seated in a classroom, and probably more effectively. A Learning Organization will have a fully equipped learning centre attached to its largest locations for the use of all employees.

9. A Learning Organization responds proactively to the wider needs of the environment
and the society in which it operates, and encourages its people to do likewise
This addresses two distinct issues. The way in which everyone can live together on this small planet while ensuring that future generations will continue to benefit from it has to be a major concern for everyone. In that sense environmentalism is a desirable part of every learner's curriculum, and several companies encourage thinking in this way. One which is headquartered on a site reclaimed from the sea on the south coast of England makes available in its foyer a sophisticated open learning programme which shows a map of the site, pictures of the principle flora and fauna and where they can be found, with sound effects so that people can listen to and identify the particular call of a bird, and videos showing animals in motion and birds in flight. This is one example of responding to the environment and encouraging a responsible and informed approach to the major issues.

The Learning Organization also encourages people to play a full part in the society in which they live. It encourages learning through contribution as well as learning for one's own advancement or pleasure. The case study of twinning in Chapter 3 (pp 46–8) is an excellent example of a fruitful partnership in which employees helped to improve the quality of education in one school. Examples of programmes to help the disabled, education, commerce, local societies etc abound and many companies operate voluntary donation schemes for local charities. Whether this goes under the name of corporate social responsibility or enlightened self-interest is irrelevant – it enables responsible learning and creates new learners.

10. A Learning Organization learns and relearns constantly in order to remain
innovative, inventive, invigorating and in business
And here is the crux. The organization which does not learn in today's world is moribund and well on its way to bankruptcy, either bankruptcy of purpose and vision if it is in the public sector, or financial bankruptcy if it is in the private

sector. A Learning Organization is a living organism, always full of ideas, full of vigour and vibrancy, and full of lively people who think, act and contribute. But it never believes that it has learned enough, for if it did this it would cease to be a Learning Organization. Those managers who reject the notion of a Learning Organization would do well to consult the many studies which cite inflexibility as one of the major causes of failure and bankruptcy.

The Rover Group: a case study

The Rover Group in the UK has had a chequered history. Well known in the 1970s and 1980s for industrial strife, it has shown a remarkable turn-around in recent years, both in business profits and in the enlightened way through which it has improved employee relationships. In five years it has rapidly developed into a classic example of a Learning Organization. In the period from 1989 to 1993 the revenue per employee increased from £31,000 to £122,000. In 1994, the company was rewarded with the first ever UK Quality Award and bought by the German manufacturer, BMW, for £800 million. It is widely believed that what BMW was actually buying was the expertise behind the success story as much as the company itself. The changes in the organization have been radical. What has helped the company to create success from failure in so short a period of time? How was it done?

Early steps

In 1986 Rover began to take serious steps to ensure its own future. It learned much from its strategic joint venture with Honda of Japan in the second half of the 1980s and inaugurated a total quality improvement programme to strengthen its focus on the needs of its customers. As an extension to this, in 1989 a long and serious study of the company's key thrusts and its vision of the future was set in motion. The outcome of the study showed an even greater need for change and growth as a survival matter. The perception that rapid change and growth for the company also entailed rapid change and growth in all its employees, identified the key to the future – learning, and more learning. The creation of an environment of continuous learning for all its employees became the Rover Group's beacon and 'success through people' a component of its strategy.

In 1990, therefore, it formed a separate organization called Rover Learning Business to demonstrate to its associates and the wider public that learning was now high on the agenda for long-term success, and to develop the policies which would deliver this. The ambition and purpose of this new organization, which operated as a business within a business across all divisions and locations of the company, was to accelerate the pace of change through learning, and create an organization capable of competing with the best in the world. Over £35 million is spent each year on supporting learning throughout the company.

Naturally, an effective means of communicating the new vision was crucial to its success, and so a launch team was formed. It toured the organization informing and stimulating, making videos and presentations, answering questions and making contact with every manager and employee. The key message was stark – change or die; but the beguiling vision of the future was the picture of the Rover Group as a world-class company, well prepared, well organized and well able to take on the new challenge with all its resources pulling together. And the key to success would be through adapting to change through the development of the individual human potentials into a cooperating and continuously learning workforce. Other measures, such as the single-status employee, job security for everyone, the withdrawal of artificial ceilings and flexible job descriptions were also implemented, thus overturning many of the restrictive practices which had grown up over the years.

New definitions

On the front page of the Rover Learning Business booklet are four stimulating definitions of a Learning Organization. They are:

> 'A place where inventing new knowledge is not a specialized activity… it is a way of behaving, indeed, a way of being, in which everyone is a knowledge worker.'

> 'A company in which learning and working are synonymous; it is peopled by colleagues and companions rather than bosses, subordinates and workers; and both the inside and outside of the company are being constantly searched and examined for newness.'

> 'A company where unlearning is actively encouraged.'

> 'A company that monitors and reflects upon the assumptions by which it operates. It is "in touch" with itself and its environment and thereby adapts and changes as a matter of course, rather than traumatically, in a crisis.'

How refreshingly different this is from the traditional stereotype of an industrial organization, a stereotype still believed in many an educational and government institution. How it enhances the vision of what people are able to achieve. How irrelevant it makes the educational preoccupation with sorting out failures from successes. In this environment, everyone is a success at one's own level, with the added possibility of greater success through learning.

Empowering the workforce

The quotations above describe an enormously challenging agenda for change. They go together with a set of forward-looking principles displayed prominently throughout the Rover sites (see Figure 15).

ROVER LEARNING PRINCIPLES

1. Learning is the most natural human instinct.
2. Creativity, involvement and contribution are fuelled by learning and development.
3. Everyone has two jobs – the job and improving the job.
4. People own what they have created.
5. People need work and enjoy it if they are valued.
6. Creativity and ingenuity are grossly underrated.
7. Management does not have all the answers.

Figure 15: *Rover Group learning principles*

The definitions and principles are visionary – the more so by originating from industry. The empowerment of people, that is giving them the mental and physical resources to solve problems, make decisions and cooperate at the appropriate point of production is, in many ways, a revolutionary action rather than an evolutionary principle. If only educational organizations would develop a similar set of principles and display them prominently. It is a genuine lifelong learning, human development model.

Empowering learning

Vision is difficult enough. Putting it into practice is even harder. Several strategies for stimulating the development of human potential within the Rover Group have been established as a right. These include:

- *Job development programmes* – Courses for improving the competence and performance of employees on the job. These courses are available to all.
- *Skills development courses* – Courses to improve the personal skills of Rover Group employees available to all who wish to participate.
- *A personal development grant* – £100 is available annually to each Rover employee to take a course in a subject which need have nothing to do with the business or performance at work. There are no restrictions – it can be pottery, cycle maintenance, learning a new language, playing the guitar, tennis coaching. Its purpose is to stimulate the habit of learning in people.
- *Distance learning and Open University* – Further grants are available to those who wish to enhance their qualifications through Open University courses.
- *Team work and discussion groups* – Teams and line managers are encouraged to meet together in discussion groups at the beginning and end of the week to air problems or opportunities, to suggest ideas and improvements, to learn together and to create a spirit of cooperation.
- *Computer-based learning* – New self-teaching courses are available via computer for those people who need, or want, to update their knowledge

and competence. Every site has an open learning facility. In addition this can be used to access a computer database which records best practices from benchmarked activities within the company and around the world.

- *Coaching, counselling and mentoring* – Employees are encouraged to develop a personal learning plan (a personal development file) and a range of support strategies for assistance and maintenance of plans are available, from counsellors who advise on content and learning opportunities to mentors who give friendly advice and monitor progress, to coaches who can help with the learning.
- *Liaison with local organizations* – Employees are also encouraged to participate in local life – to become governors of schools or colleges, to offer their services to clubs and societies, to organize fetes and festivals and to involve not only themselves but all their families in these.

What's in it for the learner?

There are considerable spin-offs for everyone concerned. The following can be identifiable personal returns on investment among the learners in the workforce.

- *It improves flexible skills.* Each person has a greater range of personal and practical skills, knowledge and competencies to use either in or out of the work situation. The ability to solve problems and make decisions at work is transferable to other situations.
- *It improves job and career opportunities.* The likelihood of remaining employed is greater, whether in or out of the company. People remain more employable because they learn how to learn, and because they can develop a recognizable career advancement path, in life as well as at work.
- *It improves the way of life.* Increased learning enlivens the mind and expands personal opportunities in a wide range of subjects. It stimulates the energy to participate in, and contribute to, a wide range of personal and community activities.
- *It helps whole families to learn.* There is a considerable spin-off into family life. People who learn together often tend to stay together. Learning parents are more able to help their children and set an example for them to copy.
- *It can lead to accreditation.* And thus a greater sense of personal value and a sense of purpose through a learning pathway throughout life.
- *It can help me in retirement.* Skills learned in and through the work situation are lifetime skills. There will be no chance of being bored in retirement.

To these might be added:

- improved self-esteem and self-knowledge;
- a greater ability to discriminate between good, bad and indifferent;
- more mental, and through this, physical, energy (*mens sana in corpore sano*);
- greater self-control;

- more awareness of personal needs and those of others;
- a more tolerant and outgoing attitude with understanding and respect for others;
- enhanced adaptability, flexibility and versatility;
- much greater happiness and contentment.

This is not a bad list of benefits to be added to one's life portfolio.

What's in it for Rover?

Few business organizations do things from sheer philanthropy or generosity. There is also a very tangible return on investment for them too. Rover identifies the following in its own case.

- *Improved profitability* – in two years from, 1991 to 1993, Rover profit went up from a break-even point to £225 million and sales also increased dramatically.
- *Continuous improvement* – of both people and products, an absolute necessity in today's highly competitive world.
- *Flexible workforce* – no need to spend long hours persuading people they should change. They already know and are willing to make the necessary adjustments.
- *Associated involvement* – the movement to a Learning Organization does not just affect the Rover Group itself but also its suppliers, its dealers and its customers. The latter two are well satisfied with products which appeal and which they want to sell and to buy. Many of the former have learned from Rover's practices and are well on the way to becoming Learning Organizations themselves.
- *Improved processes* – in all parts of the workplace: design, development, production, distribution, marketing, human resource. It leads to higher quality products more attuned to the needs of the customer.
- *Survival* – speaks for itself.

We have presented this case study as an example of how one company is coping with the changing world. It sets out neither to criticize nor to extol – simply to explain. It is not the only company carrying out Learning Organization principles. There are many of these throughout the world, and they are best prepared to meet the future with confidence. But the case study has wide implications for the educational services as well as for industry. The new world of personal empowerment in industry demands certain responses from the schools, universities and colleges. If people, in the future, are to work in a continuously changing learning environment for the whole of their lives, then some serious thinking needs to be done on the sorts of lifetime skills, curriculum content and learning methodologies which these organizations encourage.

We do not prescribe a diet of education attuned only to industry and employability needs. Each type of organization obviously has its own set of needs, inhibitors and visions relating mostly to developing the whole person. But the principles of empowerment in industry do this, and there needs to be developed a synergy of purpose equally important to both sides of the divide. Schools, universities and colleges must also become Learning Organizations, learning from the experience of industry, the requirements of employability and the demands of the wider society. So much can be learned from each other, and such a movement simply strengthens the need for partnerships and dialogue across whole communities.

The Rover Group is well aware that the marketplace for cars is a highly competitive one and that its major competitors are also becoming Learning Organizations. It would be the last to claim that it has a monopoly of the truth in terms of best practice, or even that it is the complete Learning Organization. But it is certainly setting an example to others, and playing a leadership role in establishing the parameters for the learning society of the future. In 1995, John Towers, the Rover Group Chief Executive, wrote:

> 'It is essential that all our employees take up the challenge of personal development and enhance their contribution to the company. The role of RLB is to provide the materials, the processes, and the motivation to ensure the delivery of this challenge. In doing so we will create the certainty of the learning process being a mainstream activity within Rover.'

Truly the problem of a Learning Organization is to remain a Learning Organization.

Chapter 6

Yearning for Learning:
New Visions for Old, New Teachers for Old

Where are we and how did we get here in the first place?

Chapter 3 described how most countries sense a crisis in the schools and the growing awareness among parents and citizens that today's school-leavers are ill equipped with the skills, knowledge and values to meet the challenges of a modern global information society. The remedies discussed there were organizational and infrastructural. This chapter discusses issues of teacher education and how it can contribute to help both pre-service and in-service teachers understand and respond to the urgent need for lifelong learning in schools and in the community.

Schools are under continual pressure from many parts of society – industry, government, parents, the community – to raise standards incrementally in order to respond to the demands of a world of constant change. Lifelong learning increases the pressure by advocating the adoption of those attributes of adaptability, flexibility and versatility which are so necessary at a time of change. These are values and attitudes which not only make youngsters more employable but also enable them to fulfil themselves in every area of their future life. The quality of the learning they receive at school is crucial and this, in turn, is fundamentally affected by the way in which the teachers are themselves prepared to meet the real needs of the information and learning societies.

There is little profit in attributing blame for present shortcomings to teachers. In general they are not given the material tools and resources to do the job that society demands of them. Even less are they given the opportunity to develop the mental tools and resources, the skills, knowledge, perceptions and essential insights which enable them to respond with understanding and wisdom to the challenges of the lifelong learning age. This applies to both pre-service and in-service teacher education. There is a need to refurbish both systems entirely, introducing the development of new concepts, stimulating the natural creativity of people who are, and intend to be, teachers, and involving them – through cooperation rather than conflict – in the development of new approaches, new curricula, new methodologies. Teachers are but one change agent in the continuing development of human potential, but they are a crucial one. In this sense, a nation's long-term economic and social health depends ultimately on the quality of the initial training and continuing updating of in-service teachers.

In popular tradition, teachers are of two kinds. There are those who go straight from schools or universities into the teacher training organizations to take an education degree or certificate and then back into the schools to put their training into action. There are also those who enter the colleges at a more mature age having previously tried alternative careers. More recently there has been a third category of very mature people with special skills who have been laid off early from industry and who choose to spend their remaining working life in teaching – these are usually engineers and scientists with special knowledge and skills in mathematics and the sciences where there is a shortage of subject specialists. By bringing experience from the world of industry and government they are a valuable addition.

All of them go to a university or to a specialist teachers' college to 'train' – although in some countries there is a movement to narrow horizons by schools-centred teacher training. In a minority of countries teachers go into the schools straight from universities with their subject knowledge and immediately become teachers.

So a key question is whether lifelong learning has anything to say to the organizations which prepare teachers to develop tomorrow's citizens. And if so, what? That is rather like asking whether there is a role for food in the development of a child, or for a spanner in screwing and unscrewing a nut. The principles of lifelong learning are central and significant to the curriculum of the teacher training organization. A stable learning society will not evolve unless teachers in training and teachers in service understand and come to terms with lifelong learning ideas, concepts and practices, and this will stretch their capabilities, horizons and knowledge well beyond present perceptions and requirements. This *must* be the starting point for a fresh look at present systems, methods and curricula, not only in the interests of the teachers but also in the best interests of children, communities and nations.

Let us remind ourselves with three observations of how quickly the world is changing, how the paradigms within which we have operated in the past are being replaced by new ones and how the average human being is increasingly unable to cope with the daily onslaught of new information, ideas, problems, opportunities, challenges and threats.

First, the growth of science and technology has given people more freedom, democracy and information, but not necessarily the mental tools to understand these or use them wisely – nor the moral consciousness to make intelligent choices on those sensitive moral issues which affect us as human beings on this planet – biogenetics, nuclear weapons, environmental degradation, euthanasia. How can present-day teacher education structures provide the skills and understanding which prepare children to face these enormous issues – and the others which will inevitably arise as science and technology feeds on its own success?

Second, the worldwide growth in unemployment in the developed nations is now becoming structural rather than cyclical; the new workplace increasingly demands high order skills and a new definition of work may be needed for the 21st century. Do we prepare teachers to prepare children for such a different world of work?

Third, the media are being used, in ever more influential ways, to inform, distort, inspire, trivialize, challenge, deceive, stimulate, mislead, or make us ever more intelligent, bitter, complacent, enlivened, depressed, active, passive. Is it the teacher's function to develop values in children which will enable them to take control of their own lives in the face of such sophisticated media onslaughts? If so how can they approach this task?

The pace of change is instrumental in forcing educational reform. Those children who become excluded because they are unable to reconcile the education they receive with the reality of the world they inhabit will become disadvantaged, dispirited and dispossessed – and if they are in any large number, dangerously so. No developed society can afford to ignore the destructive power of ignorance. Whether they like it or not those organizations training teachers are in the front line of the battle against exclusion, and it is crucial that they have the right strategies and the right weapons with which to fight and win. The creation of a lifelong learning society, as we have defined it, is one of the most powerful of these battle strategies, and it is a huge task.

Developing human potential – the challenges to the education of teachers

These are not only challenges, they are also major mandates. If they are not addressed seriously, backed by the resources of wise government, and supported by the enthusiastic participation of a well-informed population, the 21st century will continue to wallow in the same sort of human ignorance which has made the 20th century one of the greatest disasters of human existence. We are looking here for nothing less than a step increase in the application of human intelligence – for our own survival. Figure 16 identifies ten of the major challenges to be addressed in order to make progress into a saner and more stable world. Each challenge is linked to one or more recommendations of the Action Agenda for Lifelong Learning for the 21st Century (see Appendix 1).

1. Help establish a cradle-to-grave habit of learning
Or create, and exploit, the conditions in which individuals, of all ages and from all sectors of society, can enjoy and profit from the continuing development of their own potential through learning.

DEVELOPING HUMAN POTENTIAL
TEN CHALLENGES TO THE EDUCATION OF TEACHERS

1. Helping establish a cradle-to-grave habit of learning

2. Providing leadership locally, nationally and globally

3. Continuously developing and upgrading skills and knowledge

4. Developing values – organizational, national, societal and personal

5. Auditing the learning needs of the whole community

6. Developing appropriate partnerships to enrich learning

7. Carrying out and using research that focuses on the needs of the learner

8. Making effective use of the new learning technologies

9. Creating national and international networks and using them effectively

10. Creating non-threatening and portable accreditation and validation systems

---

Figure 16: *Ten challenges to the education of teachers*

The development of the habit of learning, like the development of the skills of motherhood, is so obviously a good thing that it hardly seems worthy of special mention. But do we do either of these well or do we leave much to the vagaries of chance? The learning habit is not at all self-evident – witness the increasingly high number of drop-outs from schools in western societies. On average across Europe more than 25% of school-leavers do not complete secondary school. There is also an increasing mismatch between employment opportunities and skills availability and a huge increase in the incidence of mindless violence.

A better habit of learning exists in the developing world, where learning is more obviously seen to be the passport to wealth and status. The enthusiasm to learn on the part of both teachers and children is almost tangible. The problems there are quite different from those in the developed world, and are linked more to poverty, malnutrition and political and local power structures. They will require a different set of solutions, although these, too, involve cradle-to-grave habits of learning.

In the Action Agenda two recommendations address this issue:

- governments should ensure that appropriate programmes for lifelong learning are available, accessible to all without exclusion, and that diverse pathways to learning form a seamless curriculum;
- industry should create programmes to develop the habit of learning in all employees.

Neither of these specifically address the training of teachers, and yet both have wide implications for the way in which teachers carry out their task of developing the habit of learning in children. In simple terms of remaining in employment it is becoming more and more important that people should learn and relearn constantly in order to keep up with the rapidly changing demands of technological progress. So it is with teachers and teacher trainers. OECD ministers acknowledge that 'the quality of education depends heavily on the skill, experience and motivation of teachers and trainers. They, too, should be lifelong learners'. Observers have noted that many people may have as many as six careers in a working lifetime and, to keep themselves employable, let alone employed, they will need to learn new skills and new knowledge continuously.

Industry taking the lead in education
Teacher training organizations can learn much from what has happened in industry. In 1995, The Education Policy Group of ERT produced a forward-looking booklet, *Education for Europeans*, which presents an industry view of the need for lifelong learning. Its major thesis is that European industry must embrace concepts of lifelong learning in order to adjust its workforce to the new realities of competitiveness in world markets. It will rely increasingly heavily on the thinking, high order skills and flexibility of people at work, and these, it argues, are exactly those attributes which should be developed from an early age. In order to address the problem of a responsible lifelong education it proposes a link scheme in which education structures create a seamless process of individual progress throughout life, from pre-school education to adult and leisure education in retirement, as shown in Figure 17. ERT contends that the issue is not just about employment, or even employability – it is about effective socialization, creating thinking and contributing citizens, and developing life skills as well as technical capability.

ERT has long been concerned with education. Its 1992 report said:

'We need to completely rethink and redefine the priorities for European education – directed towards the needs of the future, not the legacy of the past. In the long term, Europe's only real resource lies in its own people. They need the very best of education and training, and the teachers and professors are entitled to ask for a clear statement of society's objectives and for help in achieving them. But society is entitled to ask them in return to be more aware of how the world is moving and more open to changing needs.'

The last two sentences are important. The world of education may be complex, but it also tends to be inward looking. Educational organizations tend to spend a great deal of time in establishing how they teach as an internal exercise in time and content efficiency, rather than learning how to teach differently in accordance with the demands of the external world. Further, their priorities tend to be affected by the expediencies of national politics rather than open to the interpretations and needs of a future society. The demands of lifelong learning challenge all these obsolescent structures.

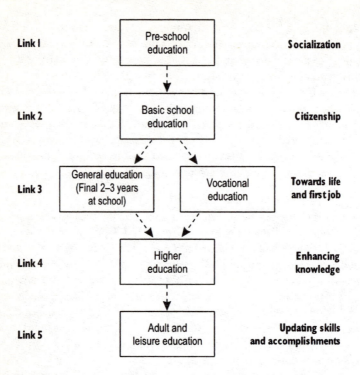

Figure 17: *The education chain (from ERT Education for Europeans, 1995)*

The case study of the Rover Group described in Chapter 5 shows how to achieve a step increase in learning ability. Teacher trainers can learn a great deal from its seven learning principles (reproduced in Figure 15 on page 81), the last of which is particularly interesting here. In pointing out that 'Management does not have all the answers', it highlights the dilemma of today's teacher. John Naisbitt in the 1985 edition of *Megatrends* made the point: 'Scientific and technical information increases by 13% per year (which means that it doubles every 5.5 years) and, since this is a self-generating process, by 1990, the amount of information in the world will be 4–7 times what it was in 1986.' In these circumstances, teachers too have to acknowledge that they 'do not have all the answers.' There has indeed been 'an alarming increase in the things I know nothing about' for us all.

One has to ask the basic question: in such a crucial area for educational development, why is industry seen to be leading educational reform rather than the educational system itself? Few universities and teacher training organizations display publicly such simple affirmations of confidence in the power of learning as does the Rover Group. It gives rise to the possibility of developing a teacher's version of the Hippocratic oath, from which the teaching profession would profit hugely.

2. Providing leadership locally, nationally and globally
This means taking a position in national and local communities in which the

teacher training organization acts as the central focus for learning activities and for leading and coordinating their development. The Action Agenda recommendation addressing this challenge is: 'Universities in particular should offer leadership to the whole educational service in addressing change'.

Consider the position of a teacher training organization within the community. Because of its need to prepare the next generation of teachers for a lifetime of change and to sensitize them to the ways by which their future schools can make better use of the vast stock of available resource, it is a natural place from which to coordinate a lifelong learning programme. In so doing it would provide a valuable service to the community in which it resides, as well as priceless insights into the real educational needs of whole communities. In order to perform this function it needs to develop contacts and access:

- to all the other educational organizations in a locality;
- to people in local government;
- through its networks, to national and international expertise which it can make available locally;
- to local industry.

It can mobilize its research facilities, its meeting and conference rooms, its staff and students and administrative capability to take on the leadership task. It can orient its projects to the development of productive two-way links which enhance understanding of the wider educational vision.

Certainly teacher trainers already have the task of giving leadership to the schools, and of creating good contacts with this, the sharp end of the educational system. The creation of a learning society, however, requires a much wider vision; to prepare teachers to prepare children for such a society demands an action-based set of joint projects and partnerships with both educational and non-educational organizations in the community, and working project relationships with national and international organizations. The involvement of the schools is also vital in the development of a learning community, and both types of organization would benefit from partnerships to bring together teachers in-service and in training in community projects.

3. Continuously developing and upgrading skills and knowledge
This means both for teachers and, through them, actions to skill appropriately the children in the schools for life in the 21st century. The Action Agenda has three recommendations for educational institutions and universities in this area. They should:

- cooperate to develop a statement of key skills and a worldwide curriculum for lifelong learning;
- encourage professional organizations to promote lifelong learning among their own members;
- help to develop a new profession of mentors, guides or learning counsellors.

Mentors? Learning counsellors? What skills are we describing here, and how do they relate to the skills of the teacher?

In a lifelong learning world the notion of the teacher, as a teacher, is already obsolescent. It is a *learning* world, in which every individual is a learner throughout life and in which the privileged people are those who facilitate that learning. The major purpose of a teacher training organization is to reorient its curricula and methods towards empowering people to empower others to learn. This is a much more sophisticated and complex set of skills, made all the harder by being ongoing, with in-service teachers, and future oriented, with teachers in training. Moreover, since it is evident that this is a process which will happen over a long period of time, there is the added complication of having to develop one strategy for the gradual introduction of the new skills, and another to explain them and why they are important.

Note, too, that the emphasis has subtly shifted from subject knowledge to skills, and not only to the skills of the teachers. As Chapter 3 showed, schools are organizations to prepare pupils for the world of the future – not of the past – and to be an effective teacher, a great deal of thought has to be given to the skills which will enable children to operate successfully and confidently as adults in a rapidly changing world. Many of these are shown in Figures 9 and 10 (see pp 49 and 50). Most of them are skills which are learned rather than taught – and a vital part of the curriculum of the developing and practising teacher must be not how to teach teachers how to teach, but to teach them how to stimulate learning and confident self-development in children.

A skills-based curriculum?

Chapter 3 suggested a turning away from the subject-based curriculum which is modelled mainly on fact retention and memory regurgitation and which is obsolete in the world of the information explosion, to a skills-based curriculum in which the focus is put on the learner and in which information-handling, creativity and understanding skills predominate.

The advocates of skills of creativity come from unexpected quarters. Many industrialists believe strongly in them, witness the top 13 skills identified from the Fortune 500 companies, and listed in the Introduction (p 3). Naisbitt and Aburdine, in *Re-inventing the Corporation*, are of the opinion that 'too many young people, brimming with creativity, are run through a system that recognizes and deals with only the linear, logical and rational side of human and social reality'.

It is as if we have learned nothing in the past 100 years about how people, including children, learn. And yet there are thousands of examples from all over the world, and in all aspects of human development, of initiatives and techniques which have enhanced learning capacity – relaxation and learning techniques, T'ai Chi, visualization, meditation, brain-storming, creativity stimulation through music, right brain exercises, transactional analysis, imagineering – all are proven techniques for stimulating the mind, increasing creativity, improving study skills and memory, enhancing performance. All of them have been used successfully in industry and business and none of them used in the educational mainstream. Where has it been in the past 25 years?

The information ladder
Some years ago Norman Longworth developed the 'information ladder' – a diagrammatic representation of stages in human development.

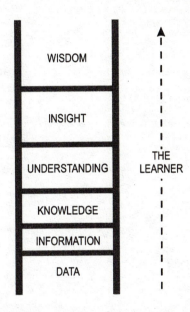

Figure 18: *From data to wisdom – the information ladder*

On the ladder one moves at the low levels from data, through information, to knowledge, ie the effective interpretation of information into a useful commodity. Many educational establishments rarely achieve even this. Beyond that, however, come steps for understanding, insight and eventually the achievement of wisdom – very few people get that far. One interesting feature of the ladder is that each step becomes wider and more difficult to achieve – a true reflection of the world of learning as it is.

4. Developing values – organizational, national, societal, and personal
The holding of lasting and stable personal and moral values is important in a world of uncertain stability. The Action Agenda puts the onus on governments: 'Governments should provide special support to families in disadvantaged circumstances to enable children to start right and to encourage lifelong learning in the home.' However, the instruments and agents of new approaches are those which governments choose and approve, and in the field of education the teachers are often the people who pick up the pieces when others have tried and failed.

The subject of lifelong learning values is large and complex and does not just include individuals. It can perhaps be approached in terms of an investment, as shown in Figure 19.

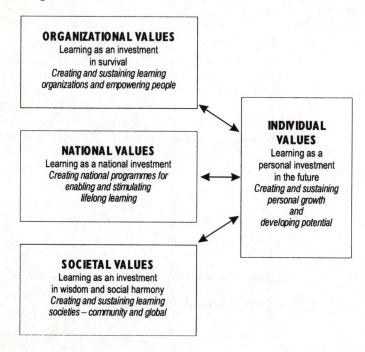

Figure 19: *Four lifelong learning value systems – investments in the future*

Thus lifelong learning values are as follows.

An investment by the *organization* in the people who work for it, the suppliers who serve it and the customers it serves – organizational values. In these terms it is a survival mechanism for the institution and it affects educational organizations as much as it affects business organizations. It is best illustrated by the power of the company culture in such organizations as IBM and in many of the Japanese multinationals. Many of these companies are proud to call themselves Learning Organizations – though many have far to go before they become one. Learning Organizations have been described in Chapter 5. Paradoxically, they are more respected in industry than in education (perhaps there is not the same urgency where profit is not the motivation?) but they have valuable lessons for organizations responsible for educating teachers.

The *nation* too makes an investment in values – a national investment. By the way in which it presents itself to the outside world, the way it treats its own people, the investment it makes in a better future, it advertises those values to all. Government plays a crucial part in the development of lifelong learning in a nation, in its attitude to education and in the leadership it is prepared to give.

Establishments for teacher training with a lifelong learning focus will have the authority to influence government thinking.

Society too invests in values, a societal investment – whether it be as a contribution to a larger global society or as a way of caring for, and liberating the creative potential of, the people within the community. In this sense it is an investment in the development of social harmony and the encouragement of wisdom. The true learning community is greater than the sum of its individual parts, and the greater the positive synergy between all sectors of society the more it will contribute to a happy and stable people.

Lastly, *personal* values are also an investment in the future. Here we are describing not only those which enable an individual to earn more – that is certainly an investment in learning – but also those which increase the quality of a person's life and make the present and the future more fulfilling. More and more the onus is being put on individuals to invest in the skills of personal growth and to develop their own potential, and the whole community is becoming a school to allow this to happen.

Where the education of teachers fits into this is self-evident. If values complement skills, and are in many ways more personal and important, then they have to be developed in schoolchildren. The ways of doing this are perhaps more subtle – often there is a powerful counter-culture at work from the media, from parents or from the peer group in which the children work and play. Thus equally subtle ways have to be found to teach them. Often an external event or extra-curricular activity – the school play, adventure holidays, school clubs and societies, sporting occasions and others – can be a more appropriate medium for implanting values than the classroom. This simply demonstrates how good teaching demands dedicated people prepared to extend their commitment well beyond the traditional school day and term, and why government should be prepared to recognize and reward those who make such a commitment.

5. Auditing the learning needs of the whole community

This means discovering what people and organizations want in terms of learning, how they want it and why they want it – throughout the whole community. The 'Action Agenda' states: 'Within business and industry each company should create a skills profile of each employee in relation to their current and future life and work.'

The general methodology of carrying out learning audits was described in Chapter 4. The European Lifelong Learning Initiative carried out some interesting research last year on learning audits. In five European countries five education providers were matched with five companies and a questionnaire was developed which asked about past experiences in education, present needs and future dreams. It did not only deal with the needs of the company but also with the needs of each individual and it covered all employees, not just the high fliers with continuing education or management training needs.

Needless to say, the results were fascinating. It certainly uncovered an enormously high, newly articulated, potential demand for education of all types – concealed because few had had the opportunity to articulate learning dreams before and fewer had ever been asked to do so. It also highlighted the perceived inadequacy of education received in the past at school, and since. It displayed a hungry desire to make sure that future generations would not be so learning-disadvantaged, but also unfortunately a resignation that nothing would improve for present generations in the near future. Above all it gave those who had carried out the audits an insight into the motivations and the latent learning longings of a wide variety of people, many of whom would not have expressed views about education without being prompted to do so in this way.

This exercise, carried out with adults but modifiable for use with children, can be recommended to every budding and active teacher, both as a way of gaining insights into what sort of learning people want, and how they want it, and as a way of restoring some faith in the value of the educational process for people who are often thought to be beyond its influence. It highlights a profusion of lifelong learning issues such as personal learning plans, the functions of a learning counsellor, personal learning styles and the roles of mentors and guides. It is another example of how industrial practice is leading educational thought, but is also a practical example of how education can catch up by participating in the collection of the information it needs to advance into a lifelong learning future.

The sixth challenge to teacher training organizations again touches on a basic principle of lifelong learning and the way in which it will develop into the 21st century.

6. Developing appropriate partnerships to enrich learning

Universities and colleges have much to contribute to society – in their capacity as repositories of a nation's intellectual capital they are a priceless asset and an assurance of its future. Working for, by and through themselves and fulfilling their own objectives, however, they become monuments of irrelevance, out of date, out of touch and out of sympathy with the world it is their purpose to serve. The same is true of teacher training organizations. The Action Agenda is strong on this point:

- each educational institution should form at least three partnerships with business, industry and community organizations;
- within business and industry, each company should form at least three partnerships with educational institutions and community education.

The issue of partnerships is of major importance. Teacher training organizations have their own natural partnership constituency in the schools and this is an essentially strong focus since their *raison d'être* resides here. This they should, and do, take seriously by such stratagems as in-service teacher training, pre-service teacher placements and supervision, joint development projects and staff secondments into schools to keep themselves up to date with changing educational cultures and needs. In some countries, this latter is a requirement, in others a recommendation. However, schools and teacher training organizations are only a part of a learning community. In the new holistic, all-embracing world of the 21st century every organization, every nation, every individual becomes both a depositor into, and a withdrawer from, the bank of knowledge which comprises the learning society. They therefore need to understand and use its assets for their own development. To keep themselves alive to the wider, real world, and often to remain economically viable as state funding diminishes, teacher training organizations need partnerships. These comprise:

- partnerships with other teacher training organizations, national and international, for sharing research and development;
- partnerships with industry to break down the stereotypes of the artificial education/industry divide and joint research into educational development and delivery;
- partnerships with professional bodies and community groups to provide leadership;
- partnerships with local and national government for joint projects in the development of learning communities;
- partnerships with vocational and adult education colleges;
- and, of course, joint partnerships with schools to involve them in the life and work of the community.

The Action Agenda specifically mentions relationships with industry as a particularly useful development and, with some exceptions, teacher training organizations have not seen the point in the past. There are many models and examples of fruitful schools/industry cooperation but teacher training organizations need to establish their own links with the world of work and wealth creation. Twinning is an excellent illustration of some of the positive benefits of such partnerships for schools, and many of these are available, and relevant, to teacher training organizations. Industry can offer participation in its courses on management, quality, personal development skills and all those topics which are becoming part of the move towards accountability in education. Many of the major new techniques and innovations in lifelong learning – flexible open and distance technologies, personal learning plans, management accountability for learning, the trend towards Learning Organizations – with their origins in industry and commerce provide valuable insights for the training of teachers. The growth of learning opportunities also offers its own opportunity to universities and colleges. People are flocking to new educational courses in increasing numbers as the lifelong learning movement gathers pace and they will continue to do so. Traditional providers must respond, as an economic opportunity, as an antidote to academic isolation and as a development of their own expertise.

7. Carrying out and using research which focuses on the needs of the learner
One fundamental feature of lifelong learning is the changed status of learning and the learner. In the past, teaching has been regarded as a process of 'received

wisdom' – the teacher passing on the fruits of knowledge to a passive audience of eager, and often not so eager, learners. The paradigm of the learning society has moved towards a motivational model of 'perceived wisdom' – the onus is now on the individual learner to learn in his or her own way. Thus the focus has changed. ELLI's third principle of learning (see Figure 7, p 35), 'The learner is the customer and the customer's needs have first priority', opens up the opportunity and demonstrates the urgent need for new research into many aspects of learning.

The Action Agenda says:

- each educational institution should apply the findings of research on the subject of learning to practice;
- universities in particular should encourage and disseminate research into learning, especially the implications of the new 'brain sciences'.

Non-university-based teacher training organizations tend to have been excluded from carrying out research. Perhaps this reflects the historical view that college-trained educators are somehow less academic than those trained at university – or perhaps it highlights the reduced status of learning research. Whatever the reason, this situation must change either by inserting teacher training into a university-based research structure or by creating new learning research centres in teacher training organizations. The last of the Learning Organization charac-teristics (see Figure 14, p 75) states: 'A Learning Organization learns and relearns constantly in order to remain innovative, inventive, invigorating and in business.' So it is with teacher training organizations. Research is one of the best ways of inventing and understanding the new future. The opportunities have never been greater nor the time more propitious. Research is needed into:

- the assessment of prior learning;
- the development of a skills – rather than content – based curriculum;
- the integration of whole communities into a learning system;
- new non-failure-oriented assessment systems;
- the development of effective self-learning strategies;
- the effective design and use of personal learning plans, mentors and guides;
- core skills and competencies for better employability;
- methods of building self-esteem and self-worth in children;
- the development of a learner's charter.

The list is endless, and Chapter 7 expands upon what each means. Teacher training organizations must play a leading role in that research, if only because they are at the forefront of its practical application in the community. Moreover, so that teachers in the schools are not isolated from these new developments and hence sceptical of them, they too must become involved in it.

8. Making effective use of the new learning technologies
Chapter 3 noted the many drawbacks connected with the ill-advised use of educational software as merely drill and practice tools in the classroom. It also described the positive ways in which schools can, and must, use the powerful new multimedia tools and techniques, and it forecast an exponential growth in their use in schools. The role of the teacher training organization *vis à vis* the new open and distance learning technologies is therefore crucial. On the one hand it has to ensure that teachers in training are familiar with all aspects of multimedia, the use of broadband communications channels based on satellite, ISDN and terrestrial delivery methods, right from the design and development of learning programmes to classroom organization strategies where they are received. On the other hand it has to devise strategies for making in-service teachers aware of their range and power and teach them how to incorporate them into their syllabuses and curricula.

There is a further role connected to such an organization's position at the centre of the community. In the lifelong learning community, resources are used for the benefit of the whole community. Thus the education technology facilities, which would best be located at a teacher training organization, could be used to deliver learning to the whole community. Figure 20 shows a simplified view of that new, community-centred role.

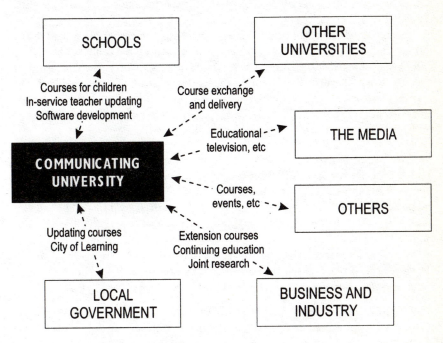

Figure 20: *The communicating university delivering education*

Thus the teacher training organization becomes the communicating organization. It acts as a resource for the whole community in the design, development and delivery of open and distance learning materials. It uses its pedagogical expertise to do this in a manner which focuses on the needs of the learner. Above all it must foster and monitor joint projects in new technology development with the schools themselves.

9. Creating national and international networks and using them effectively

If there is a number one lifelong learning priority among the challenges, this is it. The Action Agenda says that each educational institution should help create a global lifelong learning network for initial and in-service teacher training.

Chapter 3 described the exciting possibilities for learning through the effective use of national and international networks – between children, between teachers, between parents and between organizations and homes connected to the school. They can, and will, revolutionize teaching and society as a whole. Electronic communication is, moreover, less threatening than face-to-face meetings because there is time to think rather than react. But here is the real challenge to the teacher of the lifelong learning age. Children may initially say no more than 'hello' or 'my name is' – but the well-trained teacher can make such communication into a true collaborative learning experience between children, between teachers, between both together, between families. This demands special training, special insights, special skills.

Teacher training organizations have a similar role to play in education technology. Before the teachers can use networks effectively the trainers of teachers will have to gain experience on the best ways to access and use databases from all over the world, develop their own databases on a variety of topics, mediate and mentor electronic conversation into learning opportunity, especially in languages, create collaborative international teaching plans, validate at distance and carry out research with other teacher training organizations and schools.

10. Creating non-threatening and portable accreditation and validation systems

The Action Agenda says, 'universities should provide programmes which allow the accreditation and assessment of prior learning' and 'Governments should cooperate to develop a global qualification system, guaranteed by reliable quality assurance, and reflecting the principles of modularization and credit accumulation and transfer'.

Traditionally teacher training organizations have not been involved in the development of qualification and accreditation systems. However, lifelong learning is also changing the assessment paradigm in two ways:

- there is a need for much more flexible examination strategies – strategies which are non-threatening and have, as their principal rationale, to increase, rather than decrease, the confidence of the learner;
- in a globally interdependent world, there is an urgent need for greater

portability of qualification systems between nations and between organizations.

The two are quite different in their impact – but the first affects teacher training organizations the most and demands their attention and their participation. Teachers are trained to give encouragement – to inspire, cajole, stimulate, to lead and offer enlightenment. At the same time there is the self-evident need to adopt and maintain standards. Examinations are one of the few ways of doing that. Under present systems examinations are designed to produce failure in order to celebrate success – it is one of education's paradoxes at work.

But surely it is not beyond us to devise a system which is also an integral part of the teaching process – the encouragement process. This would be a system which does not pass and fail, but whose whole purpose is simply to give information and stimulus to the student, and the teacher, that learning has or has not taken place. Or it would identify that learning has only partly taken place and needs more attention, without pejorative value judgements and demeaning comparisons with others. This would be a human potential development model – as opposed to the 'look how clever I am and how thick you are' model which we have adopted over the centuries.

Again support for this view comes from industry. Figure 26 (p 127) shows five characteristics of the learning society published by ERT. Number 3 recommends that in a learning society 'assessment confirms progress rather than brands failure'. The new lifelong learning paradigm demands the eradication of alienation, the end to failure, the celebration of learning – and, as it is expressed in business terms, a win–win situation. There is a new holism in the world of education, as there is in the world of environmental protection, technology management and engineering. It is caused by the rapidly developing trend to lifelong learning, and all these challenges are central to that holistic philosophy.

Transforming teacher training organizations

The challenges, once met, will radically transform the role and the practice of teacher training. Just one challenge remains, and that is to turn them into an easily understood set of characteristics that can be measured and monitored by the teacher training organizations themselves. Figure 21 is just that. It can be used as a basis for self-assessment, a list of goals for making the transformation into lifelong learning organization, and/or a weighted checklist for converting into a strategy for action.

A lifelong learning teacher development organization...

1. Creates an annually updated and flexible organizational learning strategy for developing the full human potential of each student and member of staff taking into account individual learning needs.
2. Promotes, through specific courses and programmes, a culture of quality and respect for high standards in everything it does.
3. Involves itself fully with the community in which it resides by:
   - creating active partnership projects for students and staff with industry and commerce
   - making a positive contribution to the welfare of the community's people including the aged and disabled
   - actively seeking to use the experience and expertise of people from the community in the learning process of the organization
   - carrying out learning audits and providing a central focus for leadership among all sectors in the growth of a learning community in the locality.
4. Looks outward to the world by:
   - creating collaborative and productive links with teacher training organizations and schools in other countries through the use of networks
   - instilling a sense of tolerance, justice and understanding of different cultures, creeds and languages in all its students and encouraging positive supportive action
   - becoming involved in national and international research into learner-centred methods and technologies and the creation of learning societies.
5. Expands lifelong learning vision in all its students and staff by:
   - developing, cooperatively with all sectors of the community, lifelong learning courses, seminars and activities as part of its curriculum
   - encouraging the use of personal learning plans, counsellors and mentors
   - developing creative, rewarding, enjoyable and productive learning programmes and activities which stimulate a permanent habit of learning in all staff and students.
6. Develops strategies to become a true Learning Organization by implementing the ten characteristics of the Learning Organization (see p 75).
7. Concentrates on the development of personal and leadership skills, particularly those high order skills which enhance understanding, insight and knowledge.
8. Uses modern information and communications technology appropriately, particularly in the:
   - effective use of educational and commercial software and multimedia tools
   - creative use of electronic networks in learning situations
   - flexible use of distance and open learning tools and techniques.
9. Involves itself in the development of local, national and international non-failure oriented validation and accreditation systems and self-assessment strategies.
10. Involves the schools in all of these activities and uses them as a strategy for updating in-service teachers and giving lifelong learning skills to children.

Figure 21: *Transforming teacher training organizations into lifelong learning organizations*

We would like to extend Kuan Tsu's words quoted in the Introduction: 'when planning for lifelong learning – start with the children and learn how to make learning so attractive and meaningful that they cherish it forever'. That is the challenge which teachers have pursued for many centuries. In a lifelong learning world, everything else follows.

Chapter 7

Discerning Learning: Higher Education and the Incoming Tide

An ocean of challenges

Canute tried to turn back the tide, though to be fair to him he was merely trying to show his advisers that he was not the all-powerful being they said he was. Shakespeare described the tide (in the affairs of man) as an opportunity which may or may not be accepted dependent on the individual's acuteness of perception and entrepreneurial courage. Similarly, the incoming tide of lifelong learning can be seen either as an opportunity for higher education to expand into the future or as a reason to pull up the drawbridge lest the present be drowned. Whatever the scenario, the moon of learning demand is affecting the water of learning provision and presenting all parts of the education system with challenges. Figure 22 shows ten of the most pressing areas in which higher education will have to take urgent decisions.

HIGHER EDUCATION IN THE LIFELONG LEARNING AGE
TEN CHALLENGES, TEN OPPORTUNITIES

1. Community, national and international leadership.
2. Quality of research, teaching and management.
3. New ideas on accreditation, qualifications and standards.
4. New learning research and development.
5. Partnerships with industry and continuing education.
6. Increasing number of maturer students.
7. Greater use of education technology and networks.
8. Competition, cooperation and a new mission.
9. Internal productivity and cost-effectiveness.
10. Lifelong learning curricula and induction programmes.

Figure 22: *Higher education in the lifelong learning age*

Community, national and international leadership
– a position of privilege

Ricardo Diez-Hochleitner, President of the Club of Rome, wrote in *Higher Education:* 'While resistance to change may be expected, the globalization trend is irrefutable. Accordingly, the future of higher education is linked to that of society itself – a dynamic process which can never be predicted with certainty.'

The university is a natural place to initiate, develop and maintain local lifelong learning programmes while also maintaining links with national and international projects and activities as described in Figure 23.

Figure 23: *The lifelong learning university at the heart of the community*

The practical implications of this privileged position are far-reaching and would drastically change the university's role, purpose and *modus operandi*. At the same time it would considerably enhance its status in the community by adding a wide range of additional functions to the research and teaching which are presently its *raison d'être*. It would remain a depository and developer of intellectual capital, a storehouse of basic facts and information from which new knowledge emerges and is disseminated, but its enlarged role would provide learning and enlighten-ment for a far wider constituency of people and concepts.

There is another sense in which universities would find such a role attractive. They can take justifiable pride in their central contribution to the flow of great ideas in the history of human development. Many of the world's great inventions have come from university laboratories and classrooms and major philosophical, economic, social and religious transformations have originated there.

One of the most powerful philosophies of our time is lifelong learning. Its influence in opening up new opportunities and new horizons, empowering people and expanding ideas, concepts and actions makes it a prime target for research. The university which does not want to be a part of that scene is indeed an ivory tower, fossilized, full of its own intellectual self-importance – and irrelevant. Ball and Stewart remarked, in the Action Agenda, that 'universities should treat the whole community as comprising past, or present, or future students'. How that would open up new perceptions on the purpose of the university and provide a challenge to the more entrenched and immobile. Instead of an institution for educating an elite of highly intelligent undergraduates and researchers, it becomes a universal university, open to all irrespective of background, qualification, age, or subject. If we believe in the power and the value of learning, and if we can create the sort of society in which learning is natural and pervasive, that is the way the traditional university must go. Such a change would demand wise leadership.

There is no doubt about the challenge and the opportunity for leadership. What may be in doubt is the extent of the university's willingness to change, its ability to manage, its vision to discern, its openness to discover, its dynamism to act and its humility to share. It poses radical questions about the definition, role, function, responsibilities and accountability of higher learning. Lifelong learning forces governments, society and the universities themselves to examine closely the distinctions between the university and non-university sectors, between fundamental and applied research, between theoretical learning and vocational training. Whatever the future institutional pattern within which higher learning will operate, the boundaries between organizations will inevitably need to be examined with care. Universities may choose to isolate themselves or try to define a restricted role based on ancient traditions, or they may pick up the gauntlet of leadership and use their power and their reputation to move into the 21st century.

Quality of research, teaching and management

Just as industry is developing new internal cultures by implementing concepts of the Learning Organization (see Figure 14, p 75) and linking all its practices towards the learning needs of its workforce, so the university may wish to develop its own concept of the Learning Organization. By definition, universities should already be Learning Organizations. Too many, however, do not put the focus on the learner, do not employ modern educational technologies and do not empower their staff and students, to mention just three characteristics. Perhaps the absence of the profit motive engenders a more relaxed approach to the process of producing and disseminating new knowledge, as indeed it should. But it should not prevent universities from seeking to insert quality in everything they do – in research, teaching and administration.

Some universities, however, particularly those in North America, are beginning to use quality measurement tools. Some are asking students to assess the quality and relevance of the teaching they receive and are relating this to salaries; some are setting deadlines for the completion of research and submitting it to efficiency and relevance criteria. Some are actually streamlining their administration procedures, producing operating plans, management decision-making techniques, departmental mission statements, advertising and image-enhancing programmes and benchmarking tools, just as if they were companies in industry. Vice-chancellors, rectors and principals are becoming Chief Executives or appointing them to work in parallel. And yet, although several universities have been involved in quality research, very few have developed formal continuous learning courses for their own staff in fields outside their own specialization.

Of course there are dangers in all these things, for example the undervaluing of an excellent researcher who is not a good communicator, the orientation of all research towards defined, applied outcomes to the neglect of basic, blue skies innovation, and ignoring individual flair in favour of administrative protocol. A haven should remain for the brilliantly unorthodox and the talented eccentric, and where else but in a university?

But our highly competitive world demands a quality approach to ensure continued funding. The university which gives the impression of being aloof from its clients, making no effort to attract new customers (whether they be a new breed of student from local, national and international industry, a government funding department or research foundation), is the university which will continually struggle to survive in such a world. Industry's desire to out-source education is a case in point. It demands new quality approaches (see Chapter 1), and the university which can provide them gets the business.

New ideas on accreditation, qualification and standards

'While qualification systems require learning strategies based on sound modern psychological and social principles, the pressure for change is unlikely to come from the universities. It is the enlightened and progressive wealth producing manufacturing and service enterprises in the different countries which will be the pressure points for renewal and development...'

(Stahl et al., 1993)

In a lifelong learning society the university is thus challenged at both ends of the system and in the middle. At the entry point, many universities are trapped in a timewarp of academic determinism based on a Burtian notion that those who have successfully jumped all the intellectual hurdles put in their way during schooldays are those most fitted to complete the journey at university. In this they have the collusion of governments. This is the self-fulfilling prophecy of the existing examination system in many countries. It survives by being rationalized into 'maintaining standards' or 'ensuring excellence'. Unfortunately the real world is not like that. There is little correlation between advanced level qualifications and the level of degree obtained after university, and modern day research into multiple intelligences, for example that of Howard Gardner at Harvard, tends to belie the notion of a predetermined common intelligence which fits one for academic study.

Present assessment systems are not based on a lifelong learning human potential model – rather the opposite. They are based on division, and the celebration of success for the few at the expense of failure for the many, within a restricted set of predetermined aptitudes, and as such they are subject to question. Under economic pressure many a university has taken underqualified students and suffered scorn from its peers. When these selfsame students emerge successfully at the other end one hears rather less of the matter. There are of course many with learning difficulties who would struggle in the university mill, but it is a moot point whether it is the system itself which creates and increases some of those learning difficulties. Certainly there is strong evidence that we consistently underestimate people's capacity to learn. In Korea, which has embarked on a systematic programme to introduce lifelong learning, and in France, there is an aim to raise the educational level of 80% of 18-year-olds to university entrance standard by the end of the century. In the UK there are ambitious targets for youth under the NVQ and GNVQ systems. The achievement of so many people to what has previously been considered (for them) an unreachable standard will certainly encourage a fresh look at some of our cherished preconceptions.

In many countries universities have control over the development of the qualifications system and it is they who control the design of the examination hoops. If they value standards they should, logically, do all they can to improve the standards they are trying to measure. Lifelong learning is changing the examination paradigm by creating a need for much more flexible assessment strategies. These may be target-based strategies in which examinations are used as learning opportunities and which have, as their principal objective, the effect of encouraging further learning by showing the way to self-improvement from that point. Present systems switch huge populations off learning for the rest of their lives.

Research is needed into the design of non-threatening examination systems which follow a human development rationale, whose purpose is not to pass or fail but to give information and stimulus to the student and the teacher. Strategies can be incorporated into the system to celebrate the achievement of a standard, but this should be a celebration of the act of successful learning itself, with no pejorative implications for those who have not yet reached that point. The new lifelong learning paradigm demands a system in which everybody, or as many as possible, can win. The danger to continuing university control of qualification is that, if they cannot produce such a step increase in achievement, the task will be given to an organization which can.

At the exit point, there is another task. In a globally interdependent world, more and more graduates are taking jobs in other countries. This demands that qualifications are made more portable, a course of action which is not as easy as it would seem. International efforts, for example by European Commission working parties, to harmonize or produce equivalencies for university outputs from different countries have not enjoyed conspicuous success. Unwelcome issues, but ones nevertheless included in the discussion package, are nationalism, pride, length of study, methods of teaching and sheer stubbornness. Some visible and portable evidence of a degree level standard is needed, perhaps in the form of an updatable learning passport, a system pioneered in Finland to help people find jobs both in and out of the country. Internationalization also demands a new look at the content of degrees and a much more open syllabus which includes at least one obligatory additional language and the opportunity to study through alternative approaches to learning.

New learning research and development

Professor Philip Candy, principal author of the report on lifelong learning in Australian universities, *Achieving Quality*, said:

> 'All undergraduate degrees in Australia should aim to have at their hearts, the development of some lifelong learning competencies… one of the hallmarks of the lifelong learner is the ability to take control of one's own learning, and I believe that these skills should be intentionally and progressively developed throughout the undergraduate experience so that, by graduation, the students have had experience of setting goals, researching topics and generally learning on their own.'

Lifelong learning presents challenges. Challenges are problems to be solved. Problems to be solved require research and development. Major organizations such as OECD, UNESCO, multinational industry and governments are searching for answers to lifelong learning questions. All of this should add up to a vast increase in research opportunities on learning. The 25 lifelong learning research departments in Japanese Universities give Japan a five-year start on other countries in the application of lifelong learning to work and society, and the rest of the world can catch up only through a greater degree of effort into understanding how it can work in their own cultures.

The work to be done varies, from pure research into the biological and environmental bases of how people learn, through the development of courses, case studies, curricula and strategies of how it can be implemented in each country, to surveys and analyses of learning needs in the community. The following, by no means exhaustive list, may help to provide ideas for universities to initiate requests for funding into areas where we need greater understanding.

- *Research into cities (towns, regions) of learning* – four UK cities have announced that they are 'Cities of Learning'. Many cities in the 'Educating Cities' movement, presently a consortium of 160 cities worldwide, focus on integrating the various agencies in a city toward the satisfaction of learning goals. What is a City of Learning? How does it differ from other cities? How can the structures which define a large community be encouraged to work together for greater effectiveness? This is a vast area for research combining many surveys and analyses. Its major output might be a set of guidelines and standards for the establishment of Cities of Learning, a methodology for measuring and monitoring their adherence to these standards, and recommendations for setting up a network by which they can communicate with, and learn from, each other.

- *Learning audits* – the development and use of an analysis tool which allows companies and other organizations to understand the learning needs of *all* their employees, and to sensitize them to change in the workplace. How can we know what education to deliver if we do not research the learning needs of all people? How can we discover and record it? How should adult education, vocational training, continuing professional development, community groups etc respond? The outcome could be a vast, continuously updated database of learning needs in whole populations, and the establishment of measures to satisfy those needs.
- *Developing non-threatening lifelong learning examination systems* – As we have seen above, lifelong learning demands a human potential model of assessment and accreditation for all. How can examinations be individualized so that they confront the learner, in a non-threatening way, with an assessment of present performance and a curriculum for future personal development? For the more mature student how can prior performance be assessed and incorporated into the system?
- *Using the new technologies for learning* – How can the new flexible multimedia approach be best used to enhance learning? How would it be implemented in a learning situation? How can people in industry be kept up to date with the latest developments in their field through technology? How does one set up a distance learning network from a university to a variety of partners in the region? How can networks be used as collaborative teaching instruments to improve learning performance? The opportunities in this field are legion.
- *Case studies of good practice* – Several organizations from all parts of the sectoral spectrum are putting learning at the forefront of their planning and policy-making. Little literature exists on how this is being done, what the tangible and intangible benefits are, the projects and strategies they are putting into place, why they are doing this, what their aims and objectives are for the future. There are also cultural differences between countries and regions. There is a great need for studies of organizations which are leading the way – including characteristics of learning companies, learning universities, learning communities, learning schools, learning teacher colleges.
- *Developing personal learning plans* – In the 'Action Agenda' these are recommended for everybody, but what are they? How does an individual start to develop one? What areas do they cover? Who helps them to begin, to continue? Who validates? What is the role of the mentor? The learning counsellor? The guide? Is a new profession needed?

- *Skills and competencies for a learning society* – Much work is being done to develop new skills in the workforce and for employment, but what about skills for life and understanding and skills for personal growth? What knowledge should people have to live in harmony in the 21st century? How can they be developed in the school, in the workplace, in the community, at college or university? Is a skills-based curriculum preferable? What would it contain? What skills are needed to develop self-esteem and personal worth? What changes will need to be made? How can new technologies help? Again there is a wide range of much-needed research projects.
- *New financing methods* – lifelong learning involves a great deal of new thinking and new structures but need it all be new money? Most countries could not afford this. So how can existing finance be redirected to satisfy the demands for more learning? What steps can government take to initiate learning in new disguises? How can the national, local, individual purses combine to create genuine lifelong learning structures and values?
- *Quality and lifelong learning* – Many lifelong learning programmes, especially those in business and industry, began with the drive towards total quality management. The insights gained from that process have frequently led towards the establishment of a Learning Organization. However, there are many parts of society as yet untouched by concepts of quality. There are few quality management courses for schools, universities, government departments, professional associations and colleges of adult and vocational education, still less has there been a formal policy to implement quality methods in these establishments. Thus there is a good opportunity to create new, or adapt existing, courses for these sectors and to extend quality concepts into real lifelong learning values and attitudes in the process. What would such courses contain? How would they be delivered? What strategies need to be put in place to make them work? What monitoring procedures are necessary?
- *Empowering people* – The principle of people empowerment is enshrined in most Learning Organizations. But what does it mean in practice? How does it change existing management structures and responsibilities? How can it be made to work effectively and without jeopardizing quality? What new leadership qualities are needed? How can it be implemented as a deliberate policy?
- *New roles for old organizations* – In a lifelong learning society each sector of the community will take on new and challenging roles. Universities, for example, may need to re-examine their traditional purposes and open themselves up to wider and more mature audiences. Partnerships between all sectors of society will need to be established and productive. A more holistic approach to cooperation is needed. What are these new roles for each sector – universities, schools, business and industry, professional

associations, trades unions, local and national government etc? How can they be effected?

- *Learning passports* – Greater internationalization requires greater portability of qualifications. How can learning passports help? How should they be designed to be of maximum help? How would they be used?
- *Putting the focus on the learner* – In lifelong learning the learner is king (or queen) and his/her needs are to be met first and foremost. But how do we do this? How do we equip the new learner to learn rather than be taught? How do we inculcate the values and attitudes which each individual will need? How can the teacher now fulfil the new role of enabler or facilitator? What effect does it have on the technology of learning?
- *Promoting lifelong learning* – The learning society will not happen because 'it is a good thing'. For better or worse, the modern world demands that people are persuaded through the subtle and powerful techniques employed by the media and the advertising industry, including 'edutainment'. What promotional activities can be initiated in a pluralistic society? Whose responsibility is it locally and nationally? What innovative promotional techniques can be used? Lifelong learning trains and buses, festivals, family learning events, television advertisements and shows, radio programmes, local learning events. How can today's stars (TV, sports, music etc) be mobilized to act as learning role models?
- *Stimulating competitivity through lifelong learning* – During the course of a lifetime today's schoolchildren will have many careers in response to the needs of a changing marketplace. Education and training in most countries is underprovided, underutilised and underfunctional. A full understanding of the concepts of lifelong learning from an early age is the key to future success for individuals, survival for organizations and competitiveness for nations and continents. How does one put lifelong learning into the context of competitiveness? What are the key actions to be taken in the workplace to stimulate new attitudes and the acceptance of new challenges?
- *Changing value systems* – Underlying all implementation plans for lifelong learning is the assumption that new perceptions will lead to new values. These include individual values, in which people will seize control of their own learning and open themselves to new experiences; organizational values, in which organizations of all types will recognize the importance of stimulating lifelong learning among their workforces as a survival mechanism; national values, in which governments will accept responsibility for creating the infrastructures which enable people to take up learning; societal values, both global and local, in which people and peoples cooperate to create a learning society in the spirit of tolerance and goodwill and in the pursuit of holistic problem-solving. What is the essence of those value systems at each level? How do we create the conditions under which people can learn new values without fear of the consequences?

Who should carry out this research? The first answer is of course the universities, since that is where the expertise lies. However, in a more pluralistic society, strategies should be sought to involve other types of organization and other people. Research has suffered in the past from being remote and academic. Its results have been resisted because those at whom they are aimed have no ownership of them. Lifelong learning offers an opportunity for 'whole-community action research', in which people from several different organizations participate in the interests of improving community cooperation. These are the research programmes which tend to be implemented.

Who should pay for it? First, national government has an interest in the results of much of this research and should prioritize it in its social science research plans. Industry, too, can use the information and knowledge generated, for example in a learning audit to better understand the needs of its workforce and improve its performance as a Learning Organization. Local government has an interest in creating improved community structures and would not only welcome data which allowed it to plan these, but would also be interested in participating in its collection. Lastly, many of the foundations can identify with the goals of lifelong learning and are now orienting themselves to supporting projects in this area.

How should the results be disseminated? Of course in the traditional ways through conferences, courses, seminars, learned journals. A worldwide web on the Internet would help further. But the results are of great interest to governments, business organizations and educational organizations, and there is a need for a central body to coordinate these activities. The World Initiative on Lifelong Learning (see Appendix B) has been established to perform this function.

Partnerships with industry and continuing education

In *Corporate Classrooms* Nell Eurich remarks that 'USA industry spends 40 to 80 billion dollars per year on continuing education, comparable to all the funds available to public and private universities together.'

Universities are being encouraged by government to invest more in continuing education as a major source of income. At the same time, continuing education itself is undergoing development and being subsumed into the larger concept of lifelong learning, which can entail periods in and out of education as a right for everyone, and is a radically different mission and way of working for many industrial and educational organizations. The immediate implications of this for universities are readily apparent. Apart from the opportunity for increased revenue, further education/industry partnerships, participation in local or national initiatives and a new role for many faculties and departments are also outcomes of a greater investment in continuing education. The implications of this for higher education fall into several categories.

- It is a long-term commitment. Universities will need to commit to the development and delivery of continuing education as a matter of deliberate policy and investment in the future. Having taken the decision they cannot then back away from it, since companies, the wealth-generating sector of society, will use it as an organizational investment and be dependent on it.

- It demands quality. As Chapter 1 outlined, industry has a quite different approach to education. It demands feedback, punctuality, learner participation, the associated development of high quality support materials and structures, and the use of educational quality measurement tools. It would wish the results of the education to be designed in such a way that it can measure subsequent on-the-job performance and eventually its effect on the company results. It is increasingly looking at more cost-effective presentation techniques and tools such as distance and open learning, some of which may come from international sources and may also involve the use of electronic networking and conferencing software to create feedback and forums. The same technology may also be used to access databases and other information sources. It may require facilities for on-line video delivery, with feedback facilities, to classrooms based all over the country, using special instructional techniques to master the processes. It may require the organizing university to initiate a cooperative course using experts from other universities, private training organizations and the company itself. It would look for learner-friendly assessment techniques, linked to a national, and perhaps international, standard, as well as the development of modular courses which can be delivered both within industry and within the university. It will, more often than not, wish to use its own premises.

Such a list of requirements is presently beyond the scope, both mentally and materially, of most universities, though there are several in North America which fulfil all these requirements and more. And yet it is a reflection of the current learning scene, and universities wishing to stay current, irrespective of the incidence of links with industry, will have to come to terms with the new development and delivery tools on a professional level. It will be an educational imperative of the 21st century. In evidence, Jane Bower in *Company and Campus Partnership* says:

> 'One of the commonest causes of dissatisfaction in university/industry
> interactions is the failure to meet expectations which were not mutually
> understood. It is essential at the outset of a relationship for the parties to be clear
> in their own minds and towards one another about their expectations of the
> project.'

It is not only the content-based faculties such as engineering and science which can satisfy the needs of industry for continuing education. As can be seen from the wide range of course requirements in the Rover Group (see case study, Chapter 5 pp 79–84) the humanities also have a contribution to make, as have the faculties of management, computer science, law, and the social sciences. In this age of out-sourcing of education, major companies are now paying court to potential providers of these services in the universities. Universities would not be expected to take over a company's education requirement without a period of transition. A phased transition, in which a lecturer from a relevant part of the university spends some time in the company prior to taking over a particular course, can easily be negotiated. Industry/university links are not all one-way – industry has as many educational insights to give as universities have industrial and human resource insights to offer. A spin-off from such cooperation is the likelihood of an increased number of joint research projects.

The most important implication however is that universities need now to make decisions. To give increased priority to continuing education, probably as a matter of longer-term comfort and perhaps even survival, or to withdraw. If a university decides to invest, its immediate need is to obtain a clearer picture of the opportunity and the need. Major research needs to be done into both the extent of local industry's demand for continuing education and the extent to which the local university can satisfy it. This needs some delicate negotiation both within the company training departments and around the university faculties. A second piece of research is to establish how far the university is prepared to go to capitalize on the opportunities; and the new structures, organizational, financial, legal, technical and educational, which may have to be set in place both internally and externally; as well as the new thinking which would need to be embedded into older behaviours and the internal education which would need to be done to accelerate the adaptation process.

There are hundreds of examples of universities, particularly in the English-speaking world, which have established good and fruitful relations and partnerships with industry, but many others are suspicious, perhaps because they see a threat to their academic freedom, or because they have a particular, stereotyped view of industry. In Japan, for example, industry and universities have developed along separate lines and industry has established its own means of educating its employees, including the establishment of company universities.

Three things are affecting the situation. First, central government funding for universities is being cut back and will continue to be cut back in many countries. Second, industry's urgent need to out-source its internal education programmes is bringing them to the universities to help in the process, and it is willing to pay for this privilege. Third, the new paradigm of lifelong learning encourages both organizations to look outwards and to participate in all aspects of community life. No longer can organizations who wish to survive operate as separate identities in an insulated world. They need each other and they need to help solve each other's problems.

Increasing numbers of maturer students

Most universities teach mature students on postgraduate and certificated courses and are well experienced with the problems of teaching in-service teachers, returned servicemen and late entrants into degree courses. The open universities have so far borne the brunt of finding strategies to teach in quantity the more mature students who wish to study for a degree, and they have performed this function well, usually through distance learning methods allied to a system of local tutoring.

Lifelong learning however will encourage many more adults to study and there will soon come a time when special provision has to be made in the traditional university. As demographic trends reduce the number of 18-year-olds coming into the universities and the economy quite dramatically, the slack will have to be taken up by more adult provision. Carol Aslanian, President of the USA College Board, reports that even as long ago as 1991:

> 'For every collegian under 25, there is one over that age. A college student who is full time, in residence, and less than 22 years of age accounts for only about 20% of all college students in the US. Among students who study at the graduate or professional levels, 51% are 30 years or older.'

There are some implications for other universities in those figures. These new lifelong learners include upwardly mobile MBA students, engineers and technicians in fast-changing fields, executives looking for a new career, women re-entering the job market after raising children, and a vast army of people displaced by the new technologies and by company downsizing. Maturer students who have been away from study for some time will need assistance to recover learning skills. Some will need courses tailored to their own special time constraints; groups of mature students may need courses in a place of their own choosing. If they have no facilities at home, these will have to be provided at the university. Some may require part-time residential accommodation and many will not be as committed to the life of the university as the captive undergraduate. More and more there is a new concept of students as independent learners as a natural concomitant of the transition toward systems catering for lifelong learning. It also follows that such systems will attract more mature, self-directed students with a strong sense of self and experience of the world of work.

Thus the challenge which lifelong learning presents to higher education is to adapt its offerings, both in terms of objectives, of content and of presentation to the disparate age range of its future clientele. This will put immense responsibility on those specialists responsible for teaching methods and on staff development.

Greater use of education technology and networks

In 'Lifelong Learning for Engineers in Industry' Dr Leenamaija Otala writes: 'Universities should take the leading role in developing, coordinating and using the new learning tools. As experts in teaching they should provide lifelong learning in all modes needed by working adults. Distance learning, modularity, transfer of credits, computer based learning programmes should all be provided by universities.' Christopher Evans, of the UK National Physical Laboratory, was somewhat more sceptical. In *The Mighty Micro* he wrote: 'No one, not even the most experienced and eminent teacher, the most knowledgeable educationist or the most perceptive psychologist, has the faintest idea what the best ways of teaching are.'

Much has been written in other chapters on the uses of education technology. It is a theme pervading each organizational requirement, and one which is central to lifelong learning as a solution to the problem of delivering more education, more cost-effectively to more people.

There are many good examples of universities using distance learning. The open universities, EuroPACE and the National Technological University have already been described, and outreach programmes exist in many countries, typical being those which emanate from the USA landgrant universities. Figure 20 (p 99) summarizes this in diagrammatic form. Washington State University, for example, has established links of many types to both industrial and educational sites throughout Washington state in north-west USA. As a former landgrant university with the mission to outreach into the community and to establish educational programmes for those unable to reach the state capital, the university has created distance learning programmes through both terrestrial and satellite links, and by dispersing its staff into sites around the state. These technologies have greatly widened the learning opportunities available to a vast range of people and have been welcomed where they have been installed. At the same time it has worked closely with industry, carrying out projects to survey the learning needs of workforces in many companies and working with those companies both to satisfy these needs and to provide a qualifications and assessment infrastructure for learning throughout the state. In particular it has established close links with the two major companies in the state, Microsoft and Boeing.

Technology can also change the role of the university *vis-à-vis* its alumni, especially those in fast-changing technologies in engineering and science. The half-life of engineers after graduation is reducing rapidly to the point where some of them have to be updated after one year and again each year after that. Several strategies have been proposed to ameliorate this – moves to make the university responsible for this process for a period after graduation, the establishment of wall-less faculties of engineering across whole continents and creating distance learning universities based on satisfying industry's needs. UNESCO has long proposed a European Faculty of Engineering based on the Technical Universities in each country and an International Technical University using the video outputs of existing universities to bring education to developing world universities in Africa, Asia and South America using computer conferencing systems as feedback mechanisms. The globalization of industry will give such initiatives a major push. It is in the interests of universities in the developed world to ally themselves to such activities as a part of their lifelong learning development strategy.

The university as a Learning Organization

In 1990 the Australian Senate Standing Committee on Employment, Education and Training produced a report which concluded:

'Australia is producing graduates who, all too frequently, are not familiar in any disciplined sense with the society in which they are going to practise their chosen profession, who are not critical, analytical, creative thinkers, whose education does not provide the basis for adequate flexibility, who are not sufficiently attuned to the need for lifelong learning, and who are not good communicators. In short, we are producing highly trained technicians who are undereducated in the broader sense of the term.'

Two years later the Higher Education Council in *Achieving Quality* wrote:

'It is broadly agreed that, if higher education is to enable graduates to operate effectively in a range of activities over a period of time, a lifetime in effect, and not just immediately after the studies are completed, then it must develop the characteristics which support learning throughout life.'

In Australian universities, therefore, measures have been taken to introduce more learner-centred courses, to use the available technologies more wisely and to cooperate more with external organizations and agencies. An example comes from the University of South Australia, where heavy use is made of a flexible learning centre to develop student-centred learning and a more open learning environment. Professor Kym Adey, Dean of Education and a convinced lifelong learning advocate observes:

'If lifelong learning is to be successful the students must be encouraged to take greater responsibility for their own learning during critical periods in their formative education. This requires staff to adopt quite different teaching and learning strategies. For this shift in emphasis to occur there should be an institutional commitment including staff development, other infrastructure support and overall strategic planning.'

A spin-off noted in many Australian universities which have adopted this approach is the provision of insights into a much more holistic view of education as a continuum throughout life and better relationships with the wider community outside of the universities. Indeed, at the university level, Australia is probably well ahead of any country in the world in its implementation of lifelong learning principles, as a direct result of the Candy report (1994).

Chapter 5 describes the characteristics of a Learning Organization and how one company is implementing them in its operational plan. Universities are not companies, however, and few outside the USA would want to run themselves on business lines. They have a different culture and a different outlook. But there is nothing to prevent them from being Learning Organizations – though they would have to interpret the principles according to their own needs.

In order to do so they will have to look with extra care at three key aspects of their operation. These are their internal productivity and cost-effectiveness, their curricula and their staff induction and development programmes. Many university staff still spend interminable lengths of time in meetings which could be shorter in time or are unnecessary in the first place. Many proposals for action go up the line from decision-making committees to successively higher decision-making committees at department and faculty levels until they are eventually rejected or accepted at the committee of deans or the budgets and estate committee. And then, if modifications are needed, the whole process starts all over again. Passing the responsibility down the line is not in the culture of the average university, as it is in the industrial Learning Organization.

Internal networking systems between staff, a technique which has revolutionized industry's productivity, are very patchy, still less one to which students have access, despite all the attendant dangers. Of course, university finance has not been as generous as it might have been, but then neither have innovative ways of raising it. Outside of North America and the better-known universities, alumni funding is non-existent, income from local industry is small and productivity of staff in terms of contact hours with students or research completed to a deadline is low – with many honourable exceptions to prove the rule.

As in the schools, university curricula will need to change to improve the higher order skills and competencies of students. Learning information and regurgitating it is out; handling it, turning it into knowledge and understanding is in, as is communicating, learning to study, solving problems and developing values. 'Tertiary education seeks to awaken the critical multidisciplinary minds, able to gain a thorough understanding not of a particular mass of knowledge, but rather the process of production of knowledge. Therefore it has to learn how to learn rather than how to teach' (Cochinaux and De Woot, 1995).

Many universities have started that process. In Europe, the Katholieke Universiteit Leuven (KUL) has created a development plan for the years 1995–2000 which takes into account the need for lifelong learning and of the potential for high-level professional knowledge updating. More interestingly it uses a technique of 'backward mapping' to plan the university's direction, first by redefining its mission and then by accommodating structural and curricular change in keeping with this mission. It shows the extent to which new missions often entail innovative administrative techniques to support them.

The demography of academia might well be used as an opportunity to introduce this essential shift with less burden than previously thought. Between 1995 and 2005, dependent on the national system concerned, between one-third and one-half of those presently in post will retire. These ten years constitute a 'window' during which academia should develop new induction programmes for the new recruits in anticipation of their changed future role.

Competition, cooperation and a new mission

The European Commission has produced a number of interesting booklets on aspects of higher education. One such, *European Higher Education–Industry Coop-*

eration, deals with the thorny question of industry research at universities. It concludes: 'The centre of gravity for research-based training is moving towards the intersections between academic and industrial milieux. Thus the training meets common needs and serves to create or reinforce a common scientific and technological culture.'

Universities are not alone in their mission to provide high-level education and research. Many companies have highly respected research and development departments where some of the major breakthroughs in research have originated. Three Nobel prizes in Physics, for example, have gone to scientists employed by IBM in recent years and other companies have claimed similar accolades. While most reputable companies still adhere to the principle of openness in publishing results of research, the increased pressure to gain competitive advantage by some is, regrettably, reducing the likelihood of this happening in the future.

In other spheres of human endeavour, too, universities and educational organizations are falling behind. The use of educational technology is a case in point. Driven by the need to deliver education cost-effectively, companies have invested in sophisticated tutored educational broadcasting systems. The ISEN (Integrated Services Education Network) was developed in industry in the mid-1980s to rationalize, design and deliver education from a central point. The lecturer, who needs to be specially trained to operate in this way, controls a sophisticated array of educational technology tools and has video screen feedback from each classroom. Tutored Video Instruction, the generic name for the technique, is more teaching than learning, but gradually the talking head technology is being replaced by more sophisticated approaches which involve the learner interactively, and there is a movement towards understanding the needs of those in receipt of the learning.

Of course, much of this work is done in cooperation with the universities. Industry research laboratories and science centres encourage the participation of university staff and work with them. In this way expertise is brought back into the university and the company gains a year or more of the lecturer's time. Much more of this is likely to happen in the future as university budgets for expensive equipment tighten and as industry budgets for expensive experts also tighten. But occasionally the university will have to proact and suggest to industry that a certain line of research could be mutually beneficial. The opportunities are there, especially in the move to a learning society.

It is, after all, the university's traditional mission to carry out research. Industry is not going to replace that role. Highly qualified graduates and researchers are the life blood of industry, above all when other countries are also seeking to improve their economic fortunes. The sharing of a lifelong learning research mission with industry need not dilute this function. Indeed, by enlightened programmes, it can enhance it and radically expand the intellectual storehouse.

Surfing the international dimension

Discussion has focused so far principally on the place of higher education in the national and community setting, and this is because it will naturally take into account the needs and interests of the citizens of the particular nation in which it is set. But higher education, particularly in its scientific and technical fields, is increasingly a part, as well as a creator, of the global economy. With the power of multimedia at its disposal for realizing human potential and linking individuals to information, so too does lifelong learning have this same potential for outreach. In short, to a far greater extent than at any time in the history of higher education, both it and lifelong learning are on convergent courses. New electronic channels of communication open up the possibilities of knowledge transfer beyond the nation state. Higher education organizations are uniquely positioned to take advantage of this both by exporting their expertise and knowledge and by importing international knowledge and practice to the benefit of nations and communities.

But if mass communication technology has the potential to forge new communities between the nation and across nations, and has the possibility to enrich the experience of individuals within those communities, it also has the counter-capacity of emphasizing the isolated condition of those individuals and nations which do not have the resources and infrastructure to link into these electronic knowledge trade routes. Thus technological progress has also the damaging potential to exacerbate the sense of relative deprivation among those who have not, be they individual nations or individual citizens. This is an important issue and must be addressed.

While we have made a strong case for the acceptance of lifelong learning principles in all countries, we cannot take for granted at an international level that all nations are ready to embrace them. Some do not have the resources, nor others the ability because of political or religious opposition. In many states the condition of higher education is so fragile, and that of academic staff so precarious, that mass higher education on a scale attained by the developed world lies far in the future.

Such a situation raises the question of whether the development of lifelong learning systems should be an instrument for the redistribution of foreign aid resources. This would entail an infrastructure and a methodology of transferring both money and knowledge from North to South using lifelong learning as a rationale for developing better educational provision, and using the universities as instruments of that redistribution. This would entail some innovative thinking on how that might be achieved. Since lifelong learning is still an underdeveloped system in many of the advanced country universities, perhaps an appropriate way of satisfying the needs of organizations in the developed and developing world together would be to establish a twinning type link. If industry could be persuaded to join in as it globalizes and has a need for learning in an educationally poor part of the world, so much the better.

The model might look something like that portrayed in Figure 24. It would need to be funded internationally, but would surely be an attractive way of ensuring the success of projects through learning.

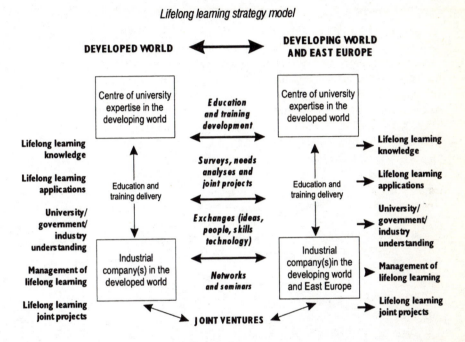

Figure 24: *Infrastructure model for university–industry partnerships with developing countries*

The model allows for the fact that in a global lifelong learning market there is a need for a core curriculum of lifelong learning. This curriculum, together with more focused applications, could be offered by several universities, working together in different continents and it could serve, for example, as part of a lifelong learning programme or a continuing professional development programme in the educational sector and of human resource development people in the private sector. Other subject areas such as quality, environmental protection and administration could usefully follow the same model for a more sustainable transfer of knowledge and skills, to the benefit of both industry and higher education.

Chapter 8

Burning for Learning:
Lifelong Learning and the Quality of Life

Think globally, act locally – the learning community

'The Information Society… must be completed and matched by a Learning Society, if we do not want to fall into an over-informed world and a valueless culture based on "zapping" and "patchwork" superficiality.'

(Cochinaux and De Woot, 1995)

The information society is with us and has been challenging us to understand and use it creatively for several years. The learning society, which provides the means of doing this, is imminent. It provides a structural framework for action at the local level, and a mental framework for understanding and action at the global level. In its most expansive form, it encourages people to react positively to global events and to develop a sense of history. Think globally – act locally, a phrase well used in environmental terminology, is equally appropriate to lifelong learning. This chapter therefore both introduces new concepts and draws together the threads of previous chapters into a set of actions to stimulate the wider vision of a learning society.

One of the most effective ways to create a learning society is first to create learning communities – cities, towns, villages or regions which harness and integrate their economic, political, educational and environmental structures toward developing the talents and human potential of all their citizens. Thus the development of guidelines by which learning communities can be established and sustained must be one of the major pillars on which lifelong learning progress can be built. Figure 25 expresses the holism behind this concept.

As communities grow into lifelong learning communities the interactions and interdependencies between the different sectors will become more marked, more urgent and more fruitful. In such a situation the skills of leadership are vital. The process of establishing a learning community offers substantial benefits and opportunities for everyone but it needs inspirational management and a communicated sense of purpose and direction, preferably using modern communications technology and media support. The symbiosis of mutual interest lies at the heart of the learning community. It promotes productive partnerships and the development of projects which aim to improve learning opportunities. Thus, lifelong learning encourages interaction between international and local, public and private, educational and industrial, government and people as essential components. They need to be nurtured and fostered with care, commitment, cooperative intent and enlightened education for all within a caring community.

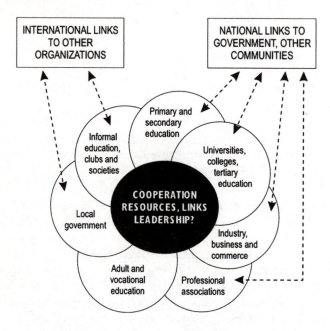

Figure 25: *An integrated lifelong learning community*

True learning communities are outward looking. Intolerance and parochialism have no place there. People moving from one community to another should be able to recognize in each the ambience of learning and use it as a means of integration. Similarly, no one community will have a monopoly of knowledge. A learning community is not closed – it enriches itself through experiences, knowledge and insights drawn from other places, other continents. The new networking technologies help in this. International electronic mail and interest forum networks have existed in business and industry and universities for some time. Their expansion into links between third-age pensioners, children in schools, professional organizations, environmental interest groups and town councillors, to name but a few, will help break down cultural and age barriers. Such links are exciting and innovative, and they open up real possibilities for understanding and cooperation, but people may need some help and encouragement from specially trained leaders. The old axiom about travel broadening the mind is accurate only so long as the traveller leaves the door to the mind open – so it is with the electronic traveller.

A learning community would also be a caring community. It would have to make special provision for the slow learner and the late developer, the eccentric and the deranged, the damaged and the desperate. In time, with greater knowledge and better remedial help and support programmes, the number of those with special needs and difficulties will reduce, but a true caring society is not diverted by pejorative value judgements, and there must always be room for the right to be different.

Towards a learning society

An aggregation of learning communities might give rise to the concept of a learning society. So how can we define a learning society? What are its characteristics? ERT offers five principles for a learning society, shown in Figure 26.

FIVE ERT CHARACTERISTICS OF A LEARNING SOCIETY

A learning society would be one in which:

1. Learning is accepted as a continuing activity throughout life.
2. Learners take responsibility for their own progress.
3. Assessment confirms progress rather than brands failure.
4. Capability, personal and shared values and team working are recognized equally with the pursuit of knowledge.
5. Learning is a partnership between students, parents, teachers, employers and the community, who all work together to improve performance.

Source: Cochinaux and De Woot (1995)

Figure 26: *Five ERT characteristics of a learning society*

ELLI has added five others.

FIVE MORE ELLI CHARACTERISTICS OF A LEARNING SOCIETY

6. Everyone accepts some responsibility for the learning of others.
7. Men, women, the disabled and minority groups have equal access to learning opportunities.
8. Learning is seen as creative, rewarding and enjoyable.
9. Learning is outward looking, mind opening and promotes tolerance, respect and understanding of other cultures, creeds, races and traditions.
10. Learning is frequently celebrated individually, in families, in the community and in the wider world

---

Figure 27: *Five more ELLI characteristics of a learning society*

These are consistent with the major themes so far discussed in this chapter for both learning societies and learning communities.

Skills for employment or skills for employability?

'Uncertainty and turbulence are the essence of the contemporary scene – and a capacity for continuing change the key to success. This means that it is essential to build up, by means of education and training policy, the capacity of the workforce to be flexible and innovative.'

(Commission of the EC, 1991d)

Much of the focus of the true learning society at the national level will be on strategies to promote understanding of the information society and to maintain full employment within it. Evidence is mounting in most countries of the developed world that both societies and economies are based on the accurate collection, analysis and processing of information and its conversion into usable knowledge. For example, Chapter 4 has outlined how, as the life cycle of products decreases, their replacements have to be designed, developed and produced within ever shorter time scales in order to compete in the global marketplace. This requires a knowledgeable, committed, highly-skilled and motivated work-force to employ creativity and innovation. While the new technologies create new markets, they are almost all concerned with high added-value goods and services, in which a high level of skill and know-how is all.

This wealth-creation driven pace of change makes demands on all parts of the system to sustain momentum, and nowhere is this more true than in education and training systems, both initial and continuing. The essence of lifelong learning for a country is to produce the skilled and committed workforce needed for the 21st century. In re-examining and reassessing the new basic skills and competencies such education systems take into account their relevance to industries and to society in the future. This is not back to basics – the basics have changed and the momentum is irreversibly forward. It means a revolution in our attitudes to the provision of learning and its take-up. Continuous learning and relearning must be available to all members of society, with particular attention being paid to those people and communities who are presently alienated from learning and therefore in danger of being excluded.

In particular, the needs of small and medium-sized enterprises (SMEs) are paramount. These companies are growing rapidly throughout the world. Many are at the forefront of innovation and must continue to be so if they are to flourish and grow. So far we have written little about them, but the continuing learning of the SME workforce is, if anything, more important to success, and strategies need to be urgently put in place to give support and full participation in the provision of learning opportunities. This is no easy task, and many initiatives have so far met with only partial success. Some form of incentive will be needed to encourage such enterprises to treat the development of their people as an investment and to establish two-way links with a variety of training providers.

Governments, vocational education organizations and careers advisers are in considerable disarray about the best course to be adopted to increase employment opportunities. There is:

- confusion about whether the problem is structural or cyclical;
- concern about the mismatch between available jobs and people qualified to take them;
- commotion about the point of responsibility, both for causing it to happen and for putting it right;
- disquiet about the cost of the resources needed to create and maintain new jobs.

Various remedies have come and gone, and some still survive – open universities and colleges for technicians, more vocational training in schools, neighbourhood training centres, training boards, on-the-job training, targets and qualifications, competency-based training, apprenticeships, career profiling – all enjoying varying degrees of success. Few have incorporated the development of lifelong learning values and attitudes as a longer-term response to the more durable problems discussed in previous chapters:

- changed industrial structures as a result of out-sourcing and downsizing;
- the growth of information and knowledge through enhanced communications capabilities;
- altered ways of working as a result of new technological processes;
- the computer as a primary tool in the workplace;
- changing demographies;
- increased competition in the marketplace;
- the migration of manufacturing industry to Pacific Rim countries;
- the growth of high value and high value-added service industries;
- the empowerment of workforces.

None of these is an ephemeral blip on the graph of employment history and none will depart easily. So complex is the interrelationship between them that the emphasis has now to be on employability rather than employment – on seeking longer-term solutions rather than supplying a series of quick fixes for economic or political gain. Once this decision is made, the main questions to be answered are 'how to' questions under four main headings:

- how to change three kinds of mindset – the personal mindset which alienates so many people from learning; the organizational mindset which treats the future as if it were a continuation of the present; the national mindset which abandons its citizens to fend for themselves in a changing and hostile world, and which seeks narrow, nationalistic solutions to international problems;
- how to provide the local, national and international structures – physical, conceptual and administrative – which will then deliver to the learner the appropriate learning in the most acceptable way;
- how to provide the carrots which will attract new learners to the fold and old learners to the new educational marketplace, and which will encourage organizations to operate in the interests of their long-term future;
- how to establish guidance, feedback and support systems which will maintain momentum and continuity and to which learners, new and old, can easily relate.

Dominating the responses to all of these questions is the need to demonstrate to everyone who wants to be employable that more and better learning is the only way to ensure this, that everyone has the ability to learn, and that learning can become a pleasurable habit.

Changing the mindset – a whole society responsibility

Responsibility for tackling the formidable problems caused by the alienation of large sections of the population from learning rests with all sectors of society.

- Governments need to set a wise example by establishing flexible systems of education which respond quickly to personal, national and organizational interests. They are also responsible for delivering the truth about the need for change and for using the media to promote the development of appropriate responses. If the people don't know, they can't deliver.
- Schools, always the whipping boys for society's ills, certainly need to improve their performance in developing human potential, but they will need considerable help from everyone in every sector to help them do it. Here is where the most resources need to be put. A package of incentives to help sensitize in-service teachers to the new tools and techniques which open up learning and change young mindsets would help, as would

additional resources to help mobilize the strategic community linkages in the interests of the children.

- Universities need to apply their considerable intelligence to act on behalf of the whole national community rather than that section of it which affects their own interests. As keepers of the intellectual traditions of a nation they may care to examine the lifelong learning human potential model more carefully in order to develop assessment and accreditation strategies which enhance the likelihood of having more people contribute to them. Negative mindsets can be created overnight by failure and changed overnight by success. A personal target-based system of assessment and accreditation may be difficult but it should not be impossible.

- Local government also has a part to play. Its position at the heart of the community gives it the power, and the responsibility, to mobilize resources on behalf of the community. A town hall brainstorm to seek creative lifelong learning schemes for intersectoral cooperation in the interests of all parts of the community could yield an interesting set of initiatives to affect mindsets positively. And so would a systematic attempt to discover what the learning needs of their citizens are. Local government also has the considerable task of making education available locally to satisfy demand. It would be so much easier if it acted as the hub of a learning society, well motivated to learn and to cooperate. The 'Educating Cities' movement and the newly designated 'Cities of Learning' are a step in the right direction.

- Industry and business probably has the largest task of all the sectors. Companies have to turn learning into wealth creation and this is becoming more and more difficult as they pick up the pieces of failure in other parts of the system and try to cope with an increasingly knowledge-based marketplace. But they too have a responsibility to contribute what they can to the achievement of positive mindsets, both in their own workforces and in the organizations they can help in the community. Many of them have succeeded in doing this as they become Learning Organizations in their own right.

So every type of organization is a key element in the battle for lifelong learning hearts and minds, and each can mount an attack on ignorance and apathy. But more specific actions can be undertaken. Mindset change is a long, large and complex process. Its agenda will require more knowledge, and further work needs to be conducted on how to develop key lifelong learning competencies including literacy, numeracy, analysis and systems thinking, information retrieval, team work, social and interpersonal skills, communication, creativity and problem-solving and the use of technology. These competencies are also important for self-esteem and confidence, the prime determinants of a positive mindset. They should relate to the individual's roles in the wider society and not simply to those needed for work.

Action to create new learning attitudes is made more difficult if it is not accepted by the key groups responsible for the implementation of change and, in particular, the teachers and lecturers whose role and work patterns would be affected. Even where change is accepted (and even irrefutable arguments sometimes gain reluctant assent), a massive programme of initial and in-service staff training programmes will be needed, since the necessity is not for a change of content but for a change of methodology and focus. If vast numbers of people are to be persuaded to switch on to learning they will need ownership of that learning, and that involves a paradigm change from the teaching model which performs to its audience *en masse* to the learning model in which the responsibility and ownership lies with the individual. This changes considerably the teachers' role, their skills and their knowledge. They become learning counsellors. For many individuals, and in certain more rigid cultures, that is a hard route.

Structure – a governmental responsibility

'The decline in the proportion of young workers means that the skills of the adult workforce will become more important. Over 80% of the workforce of the year 2000 is already in the labour market, the stock of competence needs to be renewed by between 10–15% per year, and the annual entry of young people to the labour market accounts for only 2% of the active workforce. This will put heavy pressure on the need to develop the continuing training of adults whilst at the same time keeping up efforts to improve the quality of initial training for young people.'

(Commission of the EC, 1991d)

Thus, in most countries of the developed world, demographic imperatives are affecting the extent to which education and training structures will need to change the way they have operated over the past 30 years. Four are particularly important:

1. The decreasing proportion of young people in the workforce requires a constant retraining of older, more mature people and a much more flexible attitude to change in the nature of work than has been traditional in these populations in the past. One-career jobs are on the way out – lifelong learning is on the way in.
2. The stabilization and eventual fall in numbers of the active workforce will have a similar effect and encourage greater efforts to improve productivity.
3. The accelerated growth in the retired population from the year 2000 will place great strains on economies and is a reversal of traditional dependency ratios. The few will need to create wealth for the many. One response to this may be to remove the barriers which prevent older people from continuing to work after retirement age and install instead a progressive retirement path beyond the age of 60.

4.   Women are increasingly important in the workforce as highly educated
       professionals in the knowledge economy. This means that the
       preconceptions which many of them have about their role in society will
       have to be changed (a mindset problem), and this will include an
       equivalent re-evaluation of the role of men. In some cultures this will be
       especially difficult because of its implications for the family and the
       greater freedom of women to influence events outside of it.

Devising new structures for this melange of challenges will not be easy, and it is
certain that the traditional ones will not cope. What we are beginning to see
therefore, and what will have to accelerate, is the equivalent of empowerment at
the level of whole populations. Just as the large corporations have devolved
decision-making to the most appropriate level and encouraged, and enabled, their
employees to solve problems cooperatively and individually, so, in society, there
should be an equivalent empowerment and enablement of people to make their
own learning decisions. In the workplace, successful transformation to the new
mandate has to come from better information converted to better knowledge and
skills; so it is for the population at large. The only difference at the present time
is that this information is not forthcoming at the right level and with the right
impact, which produces a lack of knowledge and understanding, and which in its
turn translates into a shortage of skills and competencies.

1. Structure – information strategies to entice learning
The first element of any new structure must be information. Nor must it not just
be offered on a take it or leave it basis, but as an encouragement – an offer which
cannot be refused. The spin doctors in the advertising and television media do
this well for products, and people buy – why not also use it as a strategy for the
marketing of learning on a mass scale?
     Who is responsible for giving learning information and encouraging people to
heed it? Again the answer is every part of society.

●   National government, as its contribution to the development of national
     values which are so inextricably linked to learning, should be financing
     national promotional campaigns on television, radio and in the newspapers.
     This is an investment in the national future, just as Rover's first outlay of
     £35 million into the learning business produced future profits in the
     hundreds of millions. At a national scale the potential return on investment
     is huge. Government should be devising innovative projects such as
     learning trains and learning buses, and using role models attractive to
     particular groups of people. Figure 28 shows a list of innovative
     promotional events produced from a brainstorming session comprising a
     mixture of students from government, industry and education in Poland.

FIFTY IDEAS FOR PROMOTING LIFELONG LEARNING

1. All parts of the system should think who their customers are and put them first.
2. Develop leaders for lifelong learning in every city and town.
3. Create the new job of learning counsellor and develop courses for them.
4. Run courses for citizens in attractive places, eg ski resorts.
5. Involve well-known actors, sportsmen, singers, in promoting lifelong learning through their own experiences of learning to reach the top.
6. Run an advertisement campaign for lifelong learning on TV and by poster.
7. Develop city centre displays promoting learning.
8. Run a TV learning evening – all shows have a learning theme.
9. Organize competitions that stimulate awareness of fun in learning – crazy inventions, learning mazes, etc.
10. Design a lifelong learning logo nationally, modifiable for local use.
11. Organize courses on trains.
12. Design a lifelong learning promotional train to go from city to city.
13. Five minutes audience participation at every theatre performance.
14. Organize lifelong learning festivals in cities, towns, villages, etc.
15. Organize competitions in which the prize is a learning prize, eg free entry to a university, a course of the entrant's choice in a place of the entrant's choice.
16. Produce a lifelong learning information folder for every household.
17. Design an attractive lifelong learning badge.
18. Encourage lifelong learning cities…
19. … with a 'welcome all learners' sign at their entrance.
20. Run a competition for the national learning city.
21. Design a lifelong learning leaflet and drop it by plane.
22. Run lifelong learning competitions in cornflakes packets.
23. Lifelong learning concerts for fundraising for the learning.
24. Think up catchy slogans – 'Learning for a better life', 'Learning for earning', 'Life without learning is lifeless', etc.
25. Compose a tune for a TV advertisement extolling learning.

26. Write short plays and performances on lifelong learning for public places, public houses, restaurants, etc.

27. Design a lifelong learning lorry or bus kitted out with technology and attractive learning programmes to visit schools and town centre locations.

28. Design a lifelong learning newsletter – have a competition for the best.

29. Competition for the Learning Organization of the Year in Industry and other sectors.

30. Run lifelong learning programmes in prisons.

31. Create quality courses outlining the best learning practices for schools.

32. School, university, college of the year competitions.

33. Design special lifelong learning toys for children and adults.

34. Persuade Sega, Nintendo etc to use their skills to design a lifelong learning game.

35. Make lifelong learning fashionable.

36. Create a Stars for Learning Foundation.

37. Make a TV soap on learning.

38. Have national or local lifelong learning days or weeks.

39. Find charismatic teachers, scientists etc – give them a 'learning is fun' series on TV.

40. Involve the press in finding a learning superstar.

41. Radio programmes on lifelong learning in history.

42. Encourage street theatre performances to point people to learning.

43. Design lifelong learning clothing – T-shirts, hats, underwear, etc.

44. Networks to put kids in contact with their idols – but with an educational message.

45. Run a Teacher of the Year competition – which children promote, run and judge.

46. Create a network of lifelong learning centres in each town and network them.

47. Promote educational tourism.

48. Find a popular politician to champion lifelong learning and be put in charge of development.

49. Let 'page 3' become the learning page.

50. Establish a lifelong learning unit in every government department.

Figure 28: *Fifty ideas for promoting lifelong learning*

While cultures may be different, and some ideas a little wild and inappropriate, as is common in brainstorming, governments may find the germs of a policy for promoting lifelong learning here.

- Some of the suggestions in Figure 28 also apply to local government. Building structures and disseminating information are a large part of their responsibility and, in their mission to construct a learning community, they will work closely with organizations in their own locality to determine what learning is required, where and when. In the new flexible world of learning their difficult task is to satisfy all the conflicting demands made by the doubling, trebling, or even more, of learners in their areas. Where other countries have constructed sports centres in towns and cities, Japan has purpose-built lifelong learning centres in its prefectures, which include sports facilities, but also drama halls, film studios, meditation centres, feedback classrooms etc to cope with this massive increase. Some are privately built and run and others are public institutions.

- All educational organizations are in the business of information giving and marketing. The schools of the future now have the task of informing a newly empowered constituency of parents and others in the community how they work, how they are relevant to both the community and the world of work and how they can incorporate them into their learning programmes. It will take some time before this happens; in most instances the present commitment is confined to explaining the examination system, how the curriculum is designed to accommodate their peculiarities and how their students are being prepared to jump, or not to jump, over the hurdles set in front of them. A more discerning audience will also demand relevance to future life, longer-term skills and competency development and an attractive learning, rather than teaching, environment. That is the external requirement – the internal one will entail proactive strategies to involve children in understanding the information they receive and giving them some ownership of the process of turning it into knowledge and understanding.

- That part of the system dealing with adult and vocational education, and with undergraduates and postgraduates, will also need to play its part in the information spreading process. It too has a responsibility to show how courses meet the needs of the empowered world, how they can be adapted to individual learners and how they would help self-learners achieve their goals. These are the organizations which should know most about the new tools and techniques and be able to explain them. In theory, too, they can use their knowledge of the psychology of the learner, and what would inspire learning and what would not. In this capacity they can take leadership of the information dissemination process as agents of local and national government and as consultants to industry. But long-term demographic change forces them to offer seductive packages to prospective students, and to do this they would have to communicate much more closely with their potential clients in industry and the public services.

- Industry may, in the short term, need to take on more of this task than it would wish. The large companies have a vital interest in creating learning habits. They have a great deal of experience in communicating with an empowered workforce and are already successfully giving information in a comprehensible format. The company which takes this process further through learning audits (see Chapter 4) will also have an interest in communicating learning needs to other agencies in the locality. However, such work is likely to be out-sourced in the future to private communications organizations or educational institutions. SMEs have always had a problem both in finding learning tailored to their specific needs and in finding the time for their staff to take it. Modern communications technology, used effectively to disseminate relevant information to those organizations which need it, can provide a solution to this.

2. Structure – ease of access
The second element of a successful structure has to be ease of access. The new emphasis on learning encourages courses to be tailored to individual needs – of time, place, pace, content and needs which take into account personal learning styles. A mixture of traditional and technological, teaching and learning, what to do and how to think may be appropriate in the short term but should be oriented towards the latter of each pair in the longer term. If the number of learners is to increase, as it must, educational organizations will need to be much more flexible about where and when they run their courses and about how they present them to the learner, especially to those who are reluctant or nervous about their capacity to learn, or who have been disenchanted with learning in the past.

The much greater mobility of people is another consideration. Changes of town, and often of country, by an increasing number of people impose new challenges. These include greater standardization of courses and common nation-wide curricula, an unlikely event outside of the schools sector, and offering no solution to the problems of international mobility. Or they may involve the greater use of education technology for remedial and continuous education courses. There is undoubtedly a need for a study of national and international lifelong learning access systems. These would, like the learning process (see Figure 1, p 19), be quite transparent to the learner and offer the opportunity to enter or leave as desired. They would include provision for assessment of prior learning and credits for experiential learning. They will lead to the better integration of support systems and a focus on the individual rather than on the system.

3. Structure – assessing and accrediting learning

The third structural issue is that of assessment and accreditation, a subject which has been discussed at length in Chapters 3, 6 and 7. These two are prime causes of alienation at secondary level and more acceptable alternatives must be found which, at the same time, raise motivation and standards. Further studies need to be carried out into the key skills and competencies required by school pupils for the 21st century, and into single flexible qualification frameworks integrating both academic and vocational programmes as an alternative to the two culture system.

Creating a lifelong learning approach

Successful lifelong learning motivates individuals to participate in the learning process. A love of learning will only emerge if it is enjoyable and of tangible benefit to the individual and/or the organization. The benefit to the individual may not be simply in terms of increased income or better employment. It may equally be in a sense of personal fulfilment gained from the acquisition of knowledge or from an enhanced ability to contribute to society.

Lifelong learning should be freely available to all groups because, in the move towards knowledge-based societies and industries, the exclusion of certain groups will damage society as a whole. The same principle is true at a global level. If developing countries are excluded from the new worldwide lifelong learning movement then global society as a whole is damaged. Social and economic exclusion threatens social cohesion. Even in developed countries many groups are not only excluded from learning but alienated from it. Special incentives will need to be developed for people and communities in danger of being left behind, particularly those individuals with disabilities who are already disadvantaged.

Educational vouchers for adult learners are one way of encouraging greater participation. The pros and cons of voucher systems have generated much heated argument. They are certainly more appropriate at the adult education level. Quantity does not create quality. A sudden massive influx of reluctant education seekers into the marketplace could have the effect of either retarding or advancing the model of education from teaching to learning. More learners would not be a guarantee of improved course quality, and organizations faced with a voucher-captive audience may make few adjustments to their teaching styles and therefore reinforce its aversion to education. On the other hand education providers might be forced into adopting new learner-oriented techniques in order to cope with the increased numbers and the more basic level of the new learners. That would depend on a number of factors including the professionalism of the education provider, the friendliness of the assessment systems and the existence of learning pathways. The idea is at least worth a try. An interesting variant however might be to turn the idea on its head and offer a voucher, worth cash, only at the *end* of a successfully completed education module.

Sir Christopher Ball's 1995 study brought out three major findings.

- First, the learning pay-off can be measured in economic, social and personal terms. Ball concludes that investment in education and training is the best investment available to individuals, companies and nations.
- Second, we have all underestimated the human potential to learn. Indeed companies take a higher view of human potential than educators do, and those who expect more usually get more. Existing systems produce existing results, and if we do not like what we get we must change the system.
- Third, carrots change cultures. Effective marketing will persuade those presently unmotivated to learn, and learning is stimulated by offering financial incentives to education providers.

Consequently one of the main recommendations of his report was that financial incentives should be systematically developed to reward increased participation and higher attainment. Not all rewards need to be financial, however. An exercise in creative thinking could produce many ideas for reward systems such as: the next course is in Paris; less 1% tax; salary enhancement; free home computer (or any other goods); a dinner out for the family; a cruise; a lottery ticket; book vouchers for the next phase of study.

Guidance, feedback and support and resources

Additional funding is always welcome to the hard-pressed educational organization and there are many worthy causes on which to spend it. The quality of educational provision could always be improved by the addition of a few people in key positions, either to teach, research or administer new programmes, or by the purchase of more computers. It is a tempting prospect to think of more money as the answer to all our problems.

But we need to take a wider view of both the distribution of existing resources and the assistance available in kind from within a learning community. Adequate resources may already exist and, with further coordination and restructuring, could be redistributed to improve local infrastructures. One simple improvement in the use of existing resources or the elimination of duplication can yield impressive savings. The social budget could also help. The social costs of exclusion are already enormous, and a study of how to re-evaluate and redistribute the total budget within the system could yield enlightening results. Some countries are investigating new models of funding education and training, but without taking a comprehensive approach to include components for lifelong learning. More encouragement through tax systems could be given to enable companies, communities and people to invest easily and profitably in lifelong learning. The USA provides a model.

'American business has begun to play an extraordinary dual role in education today. In society at large, American corporations have become the nation's leading education activists. Furthermore, within themselves, corporations are… transforming themselves into universities in their own right, so vast, so competent, that they begin to rival the traditional education system.'

(Naisbitt and Aburdine, 1986)

Alternative funding models should take into account:

- the balance of funding between governments, enterprises and individuals;
- the promotion of lifelong learning as an investment and not a cost;
- the introduction of positive concepts like learning banks;
- encouragement for small companies to engage their staff in lifelong learning as a capital investment;
- directing support to the individual learner and addressing the issue of exclusion.

Other aspects of guidance and support are worth mentioning in this context. Most informed authorities now recognize that the information explosion has rendered much of the teacher's present function irrelevant. This is not only a factor in terms of subject matter and content but also in terms of the vastly increased range of skills which learners will have to employ. As Chapter 6 showed, the teacher now has a much more important task – to develop skills which enhance learning, to have a wide knowledge of tools and techniques which allow that to happen and to know how to use them.

Thus, the new profession in the education industry is that of the learning counsellor. This is a person who is as employable by industry and business as by schools, universities and local government. In effect, many teachers will become learning counsellors. Among other skills they will have to know:

- how to develop educational software so that it incorporates the best educational feedback principles and satisfies the needs of the learner;
- how to use distance learning technologies;
- how to guide the learner through myriad pathways to learning sources;
- how to develop and maintain databases;
- how to motivate learning;
- how to set individualized learning models;
- how to develop and administer targeted evaluation techniques and personal progress modules;
- how to set up personal profiling systems; and
- where the best educational courses in a variety of topics can be found, locally, nationally and internationally.

This is the easy list. The psychology of learning stimulation, how to make it enjoyable, how to encourage creativity, how to identify barriers to confidence, how to use new techniques such as T'ai Chi, meditation, transactional analysis, brainstorming etc, might be marginally more difficult. How to open up the mind to new learning, and how to develop effective collaborative learning programmes through electronic networks nationally and internationally, would also be more challenging.

Informal learning in the learning community

Some mention was made in Chapter 1 of the range of educational experiences taking place outside of the formal education systems and the workplace. There is a vast number of people who would not describe themselves as teachers but who nevertheless pass on information, knowledge, understanding and, sometimes, wisdom. They include parents, friends, neighbours, doctors, lawyers, councillors, scout and guide leaders, political and religious leaders, journalists, television presenters, comedians and actors. When we cast our minds back to the people who have influenced who and what we are we can usually find more examples from these groups of people than from the formal teaching we received. Museums, libraries and churches are not a part of the formal system but they affect the values and attitudes of many people. They are all part of our own personal community of learning. They stimulate or kill our desire to learn.

Because the field of informal education has few restrictions placed around it, there are probably more opportunities for visionary problem-solving and innovative ideas. Figure 29 describes some of these.

- *Celebrate achievement.* The need for communities to celebrate achievements by learners is vital. Achievements are important and real to the learner. Even recreational activities produce competencies in learners that need to be recognized by the community in a way that is consistent with the local culture. A modification of the idea behind the learning passport may be relevant here. In Japan many people have their own learning and achievement record, a sort of annually updatable curriculum vitae which includes details of significant events in the life of the holder during the year. It is celebrated in the learner's own family and among the community at large. Cultural factors will determine whether this is acceptable in other countries, but the principle of celebration is worth holding on to. However, one of the greatest celebrations of learning at any level would be for learning to be recognized as a great achievement in itself. A Nobel learning prize or, failing that, a European or national learning prize, a world or national or community learning day, week or month. The creative possibilities are endless.

TEN IDEAS FOR CREATIVE AND ENJOYABLE LEARNING

Celebrate achievement	Fun learning competitions
Take learning to the people	Develop leaders
Make learning purposeful	Involve whole families
Mobilize everyone in the community	Use the media creatively
Make learning a birthright	Create spaces of learning

Figure 29: *Enriching the learning community*

- *Take learning to the people*. Existing teaching methods are often perceived by children and adults as boring, perhaps because they are traditionally confined within the classroom. The whole geographical area of a community should be seen as a 'learning field' and include the outdoors as well as the indoors. Thus the local schools, higher and further education organizations, scouts and guides, church groups, local interest groups such as bird-watchers, gardening clubs, photographic societies can unite to engage in researching local history, biology, literature, geography and produce ways of communicating this to the community. It may involve nature trails, history tours, placing commemorative plaques on doors or plans of the physical development of the community. While many curricula contain some of these elements, very few involve the dimension of communicating it to others and thus enriching and enhancing the learning. Even fewer encourage cooperation between diverse experts. Schoolchildren and adults contacting the informal system through projects of this kind can find a lifelong interest.

- *Make learning purposeful*. A variant of this might be a series of 'watch' schemes which preserve and monitor the local environment. Organized along the lines of a neighbourhood watch programme, in which groups of people keep guard against burglars and crime, the idea could extend to trees, the weather, birds, rivers, the coastline, insects, and any other project which involved people learning about and monitoring aspects of the environment. Technology, such as acid rain kits, air and water pollution testing equipment, small handheld computers could also be used to record, analyse and describe changes. National and international links would bring in new learning and opportunities for useful and fascinating collaborative work.

- *Mobilize everyone in the community*. 'Theatres of learning' might be established in every community using existing buildings and facilities. Schoolchildren, the retired and the unemployed could be mobilized locally to run such theatres, which could be linked to homes and schools through the new technologies.

- *Make learning a birthright*. The idea of a learning birthright is an important one. We have already highlighted the inalienable right of every person to receive learning – for example the principles of learning (Figure 7, p 35) and the need to develop a 'learner's charter'. The practical ways in which these may be implemented are more difficult. A public demonstration of support for the idea that everyone is a learner and all learners are born with equal rights to learning is one way of stimulating communities to develop a common purpose. All public places – museums, libraries, clinics, town halls – have their part to play in this. Local well-publicized 'learning days', coinciding with the start of new school, adult education and vocational training terms, and incorporating parades, concerts and plays, are another way of injecting fun.

- *Fun learning competitions*. All academic institutions and community organizations should periodically assess themselves against the principles of learning (Figure 7, p 35) and those of the Learning Organization (Figure 14, p 75) and there should be annual competitions in the community for the school, the company, the teacher, the local government department of the year. The judging would be done by those who have been excluded from the system – the unemployed, the homeless, the under-educated – which would provide a way of extending learning and motivation to the currently unmotivated.

- *Develop leaders*. The key to implementing successful ideas, strategies, programmes and dreams lies with people, and in particular those people with the insight and the energy to take the leadership role. The concept of leadership is of major importance in the effectiveness of learning but is one which has been neglected at international, national and local level. Local communities should organize courses to develop the learning leaders for tomorrow. For projects of the kind we are discussing, these leaders can come from anywhere in the community, from any background. They should be immersed in the skills of creativity and, just as important, how to develop creativity in others. They should run brainstorming sessions with local government officers, schoolteachers and children, the disadvantaged and disabled, higher education lecturers, special interest groups. These, in themselves, would inspire new solutions to old problems. They should be encouraged to use all the resources of the community around them – the buildings, streets, parks, theatres, shops, restaurants and public houses – to spread the message of learning and to involve people in projects to enhance it. Particularly successful leaders might be given an award such as 'freedom of the learning community' or an accreditation as a 'learning facilitator'.

- *Involve whole families*. The family is the most fundamental unit for the development of learning throughout life. Parents have a pivotal role in laying the foundations for continuous learning in every child. The breakdown in many families within the developed world is a serious issue, with learning by young children hampered at a time when their confidence and self-esteem are being shaped. Thus special programmes to enhance the role of the family in the community should be initiated. Families which learn together are more likely to stay together, and innovative schemes which recognize this fact should be encouraged. They might include joint family qualifications, family learning days, interfamily links through e-mail, the family learning album and the development of special family courses. There *are* creative ways of support and development.

- *Use the media creatively*. Throughout the world, at all levels, the media have assumed a central and powerful role in the lives of most people. Moving pictures, supplemented by words, are the source of most people's learning. Promotional events will enhance learning, especially if they are participatory and involve large numbers of people. Learning festivals could bring several thousand additional people into the learning fold. But there are many more opportunities for the effective marketing of learning at local, national and international levels. The recognition of learning achievements in others can be a great stimulator, and local television, radio and press should highlight these. In a non-failure oriented system the opportunities to publicize the achievements of those who do not normally get a mention in these circles will be enhanced. Events in the learning process could be highlighted: children's projects, disabled groups overcoming their difficulties, the work of a local interest group connected with the environment. The 'sponsored learn' is an idea which might take off. The media need to give a much more sympathetic and understanding ear to the world of learning, emphasizing positively new methodologies and eschewing the tired old learning metaphors which present memory skills as the only aspect of intelligence, or examination pass rates as the only determinant of a good school. As lifelong learning becomes more and more a feature of the community, the media will increasingly be looking for learning success stories – and, in so doing, they themselves will learn about learning.
- *Create spaces of learning*. Finally, the concept of a city, a town, a village, a region of learning should be officially proclaimed in every locality. A learning community is a web of organizations linked together in a common cause – to create a learning environment by learning with and from each other. Within the web may be hospitals, voluntary organizations, theatres, sporting clubs, museums as well as companies, schools, colleges and universities. Each of them should aspire to be Learning Organizations. A set of standards is needed to measure effectiveness in each organization, each neighbourhood, each sector, for the city as a whole and nationally, so that one can be inspired by another. A learning community would include

especially the performance of the informal education sector. Cities (towns etc) of Learning may be twinned with others and also become part of a worldwide network of similar places. Groups will link electronically with similar interest groups in the 'sister city' and learn from each other. There may be an annual national or international competition for the 'world city of learning' or perhaps a 'world learning Olympics'.

Conclusion

What we have tried to describe in this book is the end of the age of education and training and the beginning of the era of lifelong learning. As a necessary companion to the age of information it will allow us to understand better its implications for the lives of every one of us and allow the human race to develop its potential in more positive ways than hitherto. Already commentators are looking at the world as it is and predicting descent into a new dark age of the human spirit – mean-minded, aggressive, parochial, utilitarian and without the ideals which allow us to reach for a more civilized way of coexisting on this small planet.

We believe that lifelong learning offers an alternative to that bleak scenario. We have summarized the changes, outlined new initiatives, presented the challenges, offered innovative ideas. We have communicated the why, the where, the what, the who, the when and the how to. We have tried to define lifelong learning and describe its far-reaching implications for every organization, every nation and every individual. It is now their responsibility, with help from those who, like us, are committed to action, to do what is necessary to implement it. Lifelong learning is not just desirable, it is a survival issue for us all.

Chapter 9

Valediction: Learning Challenges for a Learning Age

What we have tried to describe in this book is the end of the age of education and training and the beginning of the era of lifelong learning. As a necessary companion to the age of information, it will allow us to understand better its implications for the lives of every one of us and allow the human race to develop its potential in more positive ways that hitherto. Already commentators are looking at the world as it is and predicting descent into a new dark age of the human spirit – mean-minded, aggressive, parochial, utilitarian and without the ideals that allow us to reach for a more civilized way of coexisting on this small planet.

We believe that lifelong learning offers an alternative to that bleak prospect. Indeed, we believe that it is the only alternative. We have summarized the changes, outlined new initiatives, presented the challenges and offered innovative ideas. We have communicated the why, where, what, who, when and the how to. We have tried to define lifelong learning and describe its far-reaching implications for every organization, every nation and every individual. It is now their responsibility, with help from those who, like us, are committed to action, to do what is necessary to implement it.

In this final chapter we challenge you to participate in that action. Whether you are a manager interested in the development of a company, a local or national government employee responsible for education, employment or industry, a teacher, lecturer or administrator curious about the development of the human potential in your charge, a professional association concerned with the interests of your members, or a member of the public with an open and enquiring mind, there is always something you can do to bring about this learning world.

1. Make a list of the ten most important ideas you have learned from this book. For each item on the list give two examples of how the idea can be put into practical use in your own situation and experience.
2. Persuade your immediate manager, supervisor, or departmental head to read this book, or at least selected parts. Outline what you believe to be important for the organization's development, for his or her development and for your own development. Tell them that you would like to discuss what actions can be taken at the organizational level to

implement some of its recommendations and the part that you in particular would be prepared to play. Appoint them as a mentor for one aspect of your own learning.

3. Take charge of your own learning. Make a vow to develop your own potential and accept that it has no barriers. Write down what you would like to learn and the skills you would like to acquire over the next five years: (a) for your job, (b) in you leisure time, and (c) for your family. List new topics and skills as well as extension of existing interests and pursuits. At the side of each item on the list write down, if you can, the names of people or organizations that can help you achieve these aims. Discuss the process with your family and encourage them to do the same thing. Find out what is common. Start the process by appointing mentors.

4. If you are a department or company head in an organization, appoint a leader for lifelong learning. If you are not, insist that one is appointed. Encourage the establishment of a network of lifelong learning leaders between each part of the organization. Give them the responsibility to discover the learning needs of all people in the organization.

5. Get your organization to carry out a learning audit. Encourage it to make a database of these requirements and to discuss it with other agencies who can provide the information and the learning.

6. Establish a link with a person from an entirely different sort of organization. List your joint knowledge, skills and talents. Discuss with them what each can do for the other person and/or organization using those attributes. Create a list of other talents and experience needed to grow both organizations into lifelong learning organizations.

7. Write off for the illustrations in this book (see copyright announcement on p viii). Turn these into presentations for others to understand about what lifelong learning really means: (a) for them, (b) for their family, (c) for their work organization, and (d) for society as a whole.

8. Compile a list of further reading on lifelong learning and/or any aspect of the subject, for example, Learning Organizations. The References and Further Reading section will start you off. Bring yourself up to date with the initiatives in this area.

9. Take responsibility for the lifelong learning development of at least two other people. Make one of these a young person. Find ways of finding out their dreams and their problems and act as a mentor to improve their learning performance.

10. Campaign to make your city (town, etc) into a Community of Learning. Chapter 8 will help. Contact your local councillor or town hall to get them to write to those already in place (Glasgow, Edinburgh, Southampton, Liverpool, Sonderborg (Denmark), Goteborg (Sweden) and Sheffield) asking how they intend to make themselves into Cities of Learning and modify according to you own culture and traditions.

11.   Join, or get your organization to join, an organization which can enlist your help in promoting the concepts of lifelong learning. The World Initiative on Lifelong Learning (WILL, see Appendix 2) and its regional organizations in Europe, North America, Australia, Canada, Africa and the Middle East would be a good choice. If you are not in any of these areas, start your own initiative and affiliate it to WILL. If you are, start to run your own country network for lifelong learning. Write to and for the organization. Use it to share your ideas, hopes, dreams, plans and expertise with others throughout the world.

12.   Bring lifelong learning to the attention of your local school. Show them the characteristics of a lifelong learning school (p 43). Volunteer to help involve the local community more. Act as a resource to the school. Show them the Odyssey of the Mind programme (Appendix 3).

13.   Write to your representative in parliament. Bring their attention to the importance of lifelong learning and give them the name of sources of reference, including this book.

14.   Help the media to help learning. Talk to your local newspaper, radio or television station. Encourage them to promote lifelong learning.

15.   Organize a local 'hearing' (see Chapter 1). Invite a variety of people to attend and talk for not more than ten minutes on what learning means for them. Tape it. Analyse the results, and articulate the insights it has produced for everyone.

We have described just a few of the actions which everyone can take to mobilize people, organizations, and even nations, into a more fulfilling lifelong learning role, for themselves and for others. Many other initiatives are open to those who simply release the confidence and creativity which is inherent in everyone, and which lifelong learning exists to proclaim.

To conclude, we offer what we have repeated in this book, perhaps ad nauseam: lifelong learning is not just a desirable thing to do, not even an optional extra on what we already normally do. It is a survival issue for us all as we enter the 21st century – the 'learning century'.

Lifelong Learning: Developing Human Potential

Action Agenda for Lifelong Learning for the 21st Century (1995)

Introduced and summarized by Sir Christopher Ball and David Stewart on behalf of the World Initiative on Lifelong Learning.

Contents

The 'Action Agenda for Lifelong Learning for the 21st Century' is Part 1 of the conference outcomes. Part 2 (not reproduced here) is entitled 'Community Action for Lifelong Learning for Developing Human Potential' (CALL) and details the discussions which took place in the seven sectoral strands. It contains the following chapters.

Project Activities, IACEE (International Association for the Continuing Education of Engineers)
7. *Lifelong Learning in Central and Eastern Europe*, Dr Raymond J Benders, European Consultancy Ltd

Conference Programme Director and Agenda and CALL Editor: Professor Norman Longworth, Director of Strategy and Development, ELLI

Foreword

It gave me great pleasure to open the First Global Conference on Lifelong Learning. The issue of lifelong learning, with which I have been involved since the early reports of the Club of Rome, has always been dear to my heart. Learning, if it is to contribute to the betterment of the human condition, has to be *lifelong* and it has to be *for all*. Lifelong learning for all is already an important focus of attention in our education programme; it will be the main thrust of UNESCO's medium-term strategy for the years 1996–2001.

Since its early days UNESCO has played an important role in exploring the different ways in which lifelong learning can take shape. Attention to the learning needs of adults and out-of-school youth has always been among our major concerns. In almost 50 years, UNESCO has set some important examples in the use of different forms of distance education and communication media to research those who would otherwise remain unreached.

The current emphasis on lifelong learning for all in UNESCO involves the organization as a whole. Creating the conditions for learning, freed of the barriers of when, where, at what age and in what circumstance learning is to take place, can no longer be the business of educators and educationalists alone. A multidisciplinary effort is required which, in addition to educational expertise, will call upon the specialized knowledge – as well as the capacity to learn – of communicators, information and informatics specialists, engineers, social scientists, specialists in the area of culture and those involved in the various branches of the natural sciences.

UNESCO will enter the third millennium with its new interdisciplinary project 'Learning Without Frontiers'. The establishment of a culture of learning is the main focus of the programme. It marks a shift of emphasis from supply to demand, lessening the stress on the culture of education. The vision of learning underlying the project aims at providing an answer to changes in today's social and economic realities in which the purpose of learning can no longer be regarded as simply an initial preparation for the remainder of one's life. Learning in the 21st century will be a continuous requirement. It will be the responsibility of societies to provide an environment, free of any barriers, in which individuals and social entities alike can satisfy their learning needs.

In this area, developing and industrialized countries share the same concern. In the context of the establishment of the new learning culture all nations are developing nations, so UNESCO will actively pursue the building of partnerships in its efforts to promote lifelong learning for all worldwide. Reaching the unreached and including the excluded will continue to be our dominant concern. Few parts of the world cannot now be reached by satellite or other broadband means, and a test of both our commitment and our ingenuity will be to devise solutions to what in the past have been intractable problems. In exploring the emerging technological potential we shall emphasize integrating the new in what already exists, taking the fullest advantage possible of all available means. We shall also vigorously urge that the benefits of the new global information infrastructures do not remain restricted to those who have the means to enter the information highway, and encourage the development of intermediate infrastructures through which such benefits can reach those most in need.

UNESCO will continue its efforts to advance the cause of peace and to improve the human condition. I welcome the focus on lifelong learning as an important condition for the success of these efforts. UNESCO will continue to participate in and promote the debate that will stimulate the growth of the culture of lifelong learning. I welcome the emergence of the World Initiative on Lifelong Learning and wish it well in its projects for the future. It is my sincere hope that this report may serve as a starting point for action.

Federico Mayor, Director-General, UNESCO

Acknowledgements

This Action Agenda for Lifelong Learning for the 21st Century sets out a very simple, clear, supportive and progressive strategy, for any person or organization, to enable them to benefit from lifelong learning. Read all the recommendations carefully, select those items which most apply to you, set yourself targets with dates, and you will have a clear plan for developing your, or your employees', potential. We are sure that others will be working on the bigger things to support all of us in the achievement of our life goals, and those too are set out in very simple and clear terms. No one now has any reason to wonder how to go about improving personal decision-making concerning their role in this complex and fast changing world. Many of the actions are not, in themselves, new. But they have been approved at the Rome Conference by leaders in the major sectors of education, industry and society. The most significant development of the First Global Conference on Lifelong Learning was that it brought together many networks, organizations and backgrounds, to develop the elements of a common strategy for lifelong learning. We recognize that what follows is but the first step in deepening the level of understanding in the move to a learning society, but at last we have a sound indication of what we can start to do – *now* – to move towards it. More work needs to be undertaken on targets, standards, the quality of educational technology and the integration of requirements of all legitimate stakeholders in our learning lives together.

These recommendations come from a unique conference which brought together informed learners from over 50 countries. All of the delegates were at different stages of our journey of understanding lifelong learning, but all combined to produce the first real determined steps to establishing and sustaining a learning organization. This report has been written by two forward thinkers in lifelong learning, Sir Christopher Ball and Dr David Stewart. They were aided in their formidable task by a team of strand leaders and rapporteurs who gave handsomely of their intellect and time. But the real evidence came from the assembly of delegates who spent long hours debating and determining the issues, and forming appropriate suggestions.On behalf of the European Lifelong Learning Initiative, which organized this ambitious conference, we are pleased both to thank them all, and offer their conclusions to you. Happy learning!

W Keith Davies, President of ELLI

1. Introduction

David W Stewart

'Creating and Sustaining Learning Organizations: Integrating the Development of Human Potential' was the theme of the First Global Conference on Lifelong Learning held in Rome, 30 November to 2 December 1994. The conference objective was to create an 'Action Agenda on Lifelong Learning for the 21st Century' and to disseminate that agenda to appropriate policy makers throughout the world. In attendance were 470 persons from 50 countries.

Sponsorship
The conference was initiated and managed by the European Lifelong Learning Initiative (ELLI) from Brussels. Joining ELLI as sponsors and organizers of the conference were Gothenburg City Education Committee, the American Council on Education, Odyssey of the Mind, Inc, the JUPITER Consortium, Helsinki University of Technology, Lifelong Learning Institute Dipoli and Adelaide Institute of TAFE. Conference cosponsors included the National Association of State Universities and Land-Grant Colleges, American Association of State Colleges and Universities, American Association of Community Colleges, The College Board, Regents College of the State University of New York and American College Testing Program. Cooperating organizations were the Coalition of Adult Education Organizations, Maricopa Community Colleges and the American Association of Collegiate Registrars and Admissions Officers.

Her Royal Highness Princess Margriet of The Netherlands, President of the European Cultural Foundation, was Conference Patron and the Council of Europe, UNESCO, the International Association of Universities, The International Social Science Council and the Club of Rome also granted their patronage.

Definitions and principles
In approaching its task the conference was guided by definitions and principles bearing on lifelong learning developed by ELLI.

Lifelong learning
Lifelong learning as defined by ELLI is: 'a continuously supportive process which stimulates and empowers individuals to acquire all the knowledge, values, skills and understanding they will require throughout their lifetimes and to apply them with confidence, creativity and enjoyment in all roles, circumstances and environments.'

Learning Organizations
A very broad definition of a Learning Organization was used to guide the conference work effort. A Learning Organization was considered to be: 'a company, professional association, university, school, city, nation or any group of people, large or small, with a need and a desire to improve performance through learning'. Such a Learning Organization:

- invests in its own future through the education and training of all of its people;
- creates opportunities for, and encourages, all its people in all its functions to fulfil their human potential:
  - (i) as employees, members, professionals, or students of the organization;
  - (ii) as ambassadors of the organization to its customers, clients, audiences and suppliers;
  - (iii) as citizens of the wider society in which the organization exists;
  - (iv) as human beings with the need to realize their own capabilities;
- shares its vision of tomorrow with its people and stimulates them to challenge it, to change it and to contribute to it;
- integrates work and learning and inspires all its people to seek quality, excellence and continuous improvement in both;
- mobilizes all its human talent by putting the emphasis on 'learning' and planning its education and training activities accordingly;
- empowers *all* its people to broaden their horizons in harmony with their own preferred learning styles;
- applies up-to-date open and distance delivery technologies appropriately to create broader and more varied learning opportunities;
- responds proactively to the wider needs of the environment and the society in which it operates and encourages people to do likewise;
- learns and relearns constantly in order to remain innovative, inventive, invigorating and in business.

Such organizations can be recognized by their readiness continuously to ask questions such as: Do we actively promote dissatisfaction with the status quo? Have we fiercely debated our shared vision? Do we really believe that people can learn how to learn, change, and be creative? Do we sincerely act on these beliefs? Is continuous learning identified as an overarching competence in every job? Do we know what our people know and can do? How many innovations suggested by staff members have been taken up this year? How do we react to mistakes?

Assumptions
Four basic assumptions underlay the planning effort for the conference.

1. *Men and women, animated by the human spirit, have a wide range of aspirations and interests that can be advanced through learning.* Learning goals associated with jobs are very important, but human beings are more than mere fillers of job slots. Learning for fun is as important as learning designed to increase economic productivity or enhance earning power.
2. *It ought to be easy rather than difficult for people to move in and out of quality learning opportunities throughout their lifetimes.* A seamless system of learning and credentialing is needed that puts the requirements of learners ahead of overly narrow institutional considerations.
3. *The welfare of nations and the world in these times depends upon the creation of learning societies.* Learning is the common thread that runs through the solutions to every problem and the efforts to realize every opportunity.
4. *The learning society will not happen by itself.* It must be made to happen through purposeful and sustained efforts by those who are its proponents.

Approach to task
The conference work effort was accomplished within seven strands in which participants with like backgrounds and interests were grouped as follows.

1. Business, commerce, and industry
2. Adult and vocational education
3. Higher education
4. Schools and teacher training
5. Informal education systems, the community and non-governmental organizations
6. Continuing education and professional associations; and
7. Lifelong learning in Central and Eastern Europe.

Work within each strand proceeded with direction provided by a strand chair. Strands also were served by rapporteurs whose work appears as sections in the full conference report. Strand rapporteurs interpreted their task in varying ways. Some provided a summary of discussion within the strand; others provided more reflective essays on the broad topic being considered.

Chief rapporteurs for the conference, in concert with the strand rapporteurs, determined the findings, conclusions, and recommendations that are herein presented as the Action Agenda on Lifelong Learning for the 21st Century. This agenda has been disseminated to policy makers and other interested individuals and groups by the conference sponsors.

Conference follow-up

A number of participants organized themselves regionally to continue as active supporters of the agenda. Initial organizing meetings were held by groups from North America, Australia/Pacific Rim, South Africa and Latin America. These groups, and perhaps more from other world regions, may join the already existing European Lifelong Learning Initiative under the umbrella of a global coordinating group to be known as the World Initiative for Lifelong Learning.

Tentative plans were made to convene a second global conference on lifelong learning in 1996. Preliminary proposals to sponsor such a conference were received from groups in Finland, South Africa, Australia, and Canada. These proposals, as well as others that may be received, will be reviewed by the World Initiative on Lifelong Learning.

2. Findings, conclusions and recommendations

Christopher Ball

It is no easy task to attempt to summarise the richness and diversity of the themes, challenges and actions under review at the conference, while also doing them justice and revealing the underlying consensus within this material.

Nevertheless, the main finding is clear enough. It is that our traditional and inherited systems of education and training have failed to create 'learning societies' in which everyone is motivated and enabled to practise lifelong learning. A world containing almost 900 million adult illiterates is not the 'learning world' which is our vision. What we have created so far is not good enough. Existing systems of education and training tend to favour an elite of fast learners, to focus on teaching rather than learning, and to overemphasize initial education at the expense of lifelong learning. What is required is not more of the same. If we are to reach the unreached and include the excluded, more must mean different.

In consequence, we are calling for major reform and the restructuring of the provision of education and training to enable every person to develop their human potential as fully as possible by means of lifelong learning. In the 21st century those individuals who do not practise lifelong learning will not find work; those organizations which do not become Learning Organizations will not survive; those schools, colleges and universities which do not put their students first will not recruit. Learning pays. In a world which increasingly rewards learning it provides economic, social and personal benefits which are, in principle, available to all.

The key principle governing provision in the future must be personal responsibility for learning, encouraged and enabled by the support of the whole community. Although the world is obviously made up of faster and slower learners, everyone is capable of further useful learning. And people can learn to learn faster. We have in the past underestimated the human potential for learning. A generation ago in many developed countries fewer than 5% of young people went into university-level education; today the figure often exceeds 30% and is rising. The *sine qua non* of learning is not ability; it is not even resources; it is motivation. When people take responsibility for their own learning, and encourage one another, the learning world become a realizable vision.

The Action Agenda for the 21st Century focuses first on the individual and his or her need for a personal learning plan, written down, and supported by a mentor or guide. To enable this to come about we make recommendations to organizations, business and industry, the educational and voluntary sectors, to governments, but above to all individuals, ourselves included. For organizations the fundamental requirement is the development of the idea of Learning Organizations. For governments – the threefold task of setting targets for learning, gradually transferring the resources for learning from those who provide teaching to those who undertake learning, and developing in cooperation a global system of qualifications, guaranteed by reliable arrangements for quality assurance. Quality matters. Our vision of lifelong learning implies an enhancement, not a diminution, of the quality of learning and learning outcomes, as it becomes more widely available. For ourselves, the challenge is to set out clearly and coherently the principles of lifelong learning. This report attempts to do that. They are summed up in the commendation to 'trust the informed learner's demand – and respond to it', and the touchstone question, 'Learning is fun, isn't it?'

Findings
Apart from the recognition of the failure of traditional educational and training systems, the main findings of the report relate to competitiveness, employability, new technologies and the adequacy of resources. What these findings have in common is the revelation that the shared assumptions of much of the 20th century will not prove adequate to meet the challenges of the 21st. We need both a new mindset and a new dispensation if lifelong learning is to become a reality for all. The scale and difficulty of this challenge is most clearly evident in the issues raised in the higher education strand.

When the industrial era replaced the agricultural era, sources of energy (such as coal and oil) replaced land and property as the key to prosperity and competitiveness. The knowledge society of the 21st century will discover that learning is the source of wealth, welfare and competitive advantage. We are experiencing a paradigm shift. The evidence suggests that the development of Learning Organizations is not merely desirable, but essential to the survival of companies in the next century. This is a challenge faced not only by business and industry, but also by not-for-profit organizations in the voluntary and educational sectors. Schools, colleges and universities also need to be Learning Organizations if they are to prosper.

But there is a particular challenge for manufacturing and service industries and business. It is to recognize and act on the strong relationship that obtains between learning, investment and profit. Large and small firms alike should entrust the role of 'champion of company learning' to a named main board director to provide leadership, while ensuring that the learning culture is fully embedded throughout the company – because learning (like quality) is everyone's business.

Similarly, the challenge for individuals is to achieve and maintain their own employability through lifelong learning. A generation ago in developed countries it was easy to find work with a school-leaving certificate at the age of 15 or 16. Today, employers demand the advanced qualifications appropriate to those aged 18 or 19. In the next century, most people will need the broad range of technical and personal skills expected of a graduate, together with a commitment to continuing – lifelong – learning.

While the findings on competitiveness and employability – and indeed on the failure of traditional education and training – reflect a broad consensus of those who attended the conference, the findings on the subject of new educational technologies and the issue of resources are disputed. Technology proves to be divisive. Some see the promise of a new dawn of wider access to more successful learning, using the techniques of distance and open learning. Others are sceptical, and are still to be convinced that the new educational technologies genuinely add value from the point of view of the learner. They seek measurable evidence that there is an increase in cost effectiveness when computers or television are brought into the classroom. They are particularly concerned by the growing gap between the richer and poorer nations in respect of their ability to invest in the new technologies. The development of open universities, pioneered in the UK some 30 years ago and now found throughout the world, provides a persuasive answer. So did the paper presented by Dr Brian Stanford on Distance Learning Systems developed in Australia to promote technical and further education in small and widely scattered communities.

But the introduction of printing or airline travel shows that new technologies may begin by supplementing traditional methods (the monastic scriptoria or sea travel) but ultimately displace them or (at the least) render them marginal. On these analogies, we might look for the new educational technologies to start by supplementing the teacher as an instructor, but in due course substantially to replace teachers in the instructional role, releasing them to become the mentors, guides or coaches who are so essential to both children and adults practising lifelong learning.

The debate on resources is polarized between contradictory views, suggesting, on the one hand, that education and training requires a substantial new investment and, on the other, that existing resources would prove adequate for the provision of lifelong learning, if only the existing systems or provision were substantially reformed and restructured.

The European Round Table of Industrialists' report on lifelong learning introduced by François Cornélis, for example, indicates that education has the lowest level of capital investment of any major industry today. Three strands at the Rome Conference suggested that the priority is the reform of the system, rather than an increase of resources. It may prove possible to achieve both these desirable objectives if governments can be persuaded – as proposed in our Action Agenda – progressively to transfer resources for education and training from the providers to the learners themselves.

Conclusions

Before setting out the Action Agenda it will be useful to identify five main conclusions to be drawn from the preceding argument and the earlier chapters. They are concerned with the questions of diversity, equity, motivation, reform and the role of the media. They are fundamental to the successful development of the new mindset and new dispensations needed for universal lifelong learning.

The vision of the Rome Conference encompassed common principles of lifelong learning mediated through the diverse practice of different regions, nations and localities. We must respect that diversity and encourage different groups to find their own solutions to the implementation of the common principles. It is particularly important to seek to avoid the imposition (or even the apparent imposition) of a western, or Eurocentred or English language model of lifelong learning on those for whom it is inappropriate or unwelcome. The vision of a learning society – for all, through life – must be clear, cogent and shared, but the realization of that vision will inevitably and properly vary from continent to continent, country to country, city to city.

The strand reports are at one in seeking equity in the provision for lifelong learning. This is no easy matter. There are at least three major problems: the gap between richer and poorer nations, the contrasts within any country between prosperous and deprived communities, and the range of individual experiences of, and attitudes towards, learning. Contributors recognized the probability that the development of a culture of lifelong learning, like the advance of technology, will exacerbate and increase these divisions and inequalities. Those whose learning starts successfully tend to benefit most from lifelong learning. Equity requires management. So there is a duty, alike for governments, organizations and individuals, to practise affirmative action to help developing countries, deprived communities and disadvantaged individuals, by ensuring that they receive a disproportionate share of available resources so that the gaps do not widen into gulfs, but narrow – if not altogether disappear. The test of our seriousness of purpose is the provision made for those with disabilities. Those who most need it should receive most help.

But the key to successful learning is motivation and that is why our key principle is personal responsibility. What motivates people to learn? Pleasure, satisfaction, emulation, curiosity, ambition, shame, fear, love – the list is endless. But we can help one another develop the desire to learn by offering encouragement, examples and rewards. The chapters in this book contain a number of suggestions for developing the motivation for lifelong learning – from changes in the taxation system to prizes and celebration of success. We need a thousand experiments, and a determination to persevere with whatever proves effective.

This report gives a clear call for the reform of existing arrangements in the provision of education and training but does not attempt to offer a blueprint for the system of the future. It recognizes that systemic change must be gradual, but some features of the new dispensation are becoming clear: it will not be achieved by means of tight, centralized control; it will involve the cooperation of both public and private sectors; and it must ensure that everyone gets the right start to their learning through the experience of good pre-school and primary education, provided as partnerships with competent parents. The paradox of lifelong learning is that it requires that people start right. One way of ensuring this is to tilt the provision of public funds for learning in favour of early learning. A common rule of thumb might suggest that class sizes (and student staff ratios) should approximate to the formula of double the average age of the learner. Three-year-olds learn best in groups of six to an adult, 6-year-olds in groups of twelve to a teacher, 12-year-olds in classes of 24 and so on. If public resources were targeted according to this formula, personal responsibility and private funding would combine to make lifelong learning a reality for the mature and motivated adults who would emerge from such a caring regime. Arrangements such as this would make possible the integrated, holistic approach to education, training and lifelong learning. Fragmented systems fail. The new dispensation must reflect an integrated world.

What about the media? If this is not to be 'just another worthy report' on lifelong learning it must help to raise interest in the minds of the opinion formers of our societies. Some countries are calling for a national campaign for learning. 1996 is the European Year of Lifelong Learning. What is required is a change of attitude towards learning comparable to the remarkable and recent worldwide growth of interest in – and concern for – the environment. This cannot be achieved without the cooperation of the media. And so the Action Agenda for Lifelong Learning for the 21st Century contains recommendations addressed to the world's press, radio and television networks.

Recommendations
Throughout the world, the following challenges need to be addressed between 1995 and 2000 and met or resolved during the early years of the next century.

1. Individuals should each take responsibility for their own learning and:
   - write down a Personal Learning Plan (PLP) and keep a Learning Passport (LP);
   - invite a friend or colleague to act as mentor;
   - encourage others to develop their PLPs and LPs;
   - offer to act as guide or mentor for others.
2. Organizations should each make a commitment to become a Learning Organization[1] and:
   - establish a shared mission statement including a commitment to lifelong learning;

- identify the learning process as a major business process aligned with the organization's mission and objectives;
- benchmark performance against best practice;
- explore the possibilities of publishing the 'missing balance sheet' of human resources in terms of the achievement of, and potential for, learning.

3. Within business and industry each company should:
- appoint a main board director as 'champion of learning';
- create programmes to develop the habit of learning in all employees;
- provide access to individual mentors or guides;
- create a skills profile of each employee in relation to their current and future life and work;
- progressively develop external accreditation (assessment for credit) arrangements for in-company courses;
- form at least three partnerships with educational institutions and community education.

4. Each educational institution should:
- apply the findings of research on the subject of learning to practice;
- seek continuously to increase productivity and cost-effectiveness;
- cooperate to develop a statement of key skills and a worldwide curriculum for lifelong learning;
- identify and match best practice;
- help create a global lifelong learning network for initial and in-service teacher training;
- help to develop a new profession of mentors, guides or learning counsellors;
- form at least three partnerships with business, industry and community organizations;
- value the experience of students as an educational resource.

5. Universities in particular should:
- offer leadership to the whole educational service in addressing change;
- treat the whole community as comprising past, present or future students;
- encourage and disseminate research into learning, especially the implications of the new 'brain sciences';
- encourage the professional organizations to promote lifelong learning among their own members;
- take account of the requirements of lifelong learning when recruiting, and when providing induction to new members of staff;
- provide programmes which allow the accreditation (assessment) of prior learning;
- cooperate to harness the new educational technologies in support of the learner.

6. Governments should:
- set targets for learning and monitor these;[2]
- encourage research into, and experiment with, new forms of infrastructure and new funding models to promote lifelong learning;
- gradually and progressively transfer the resources for learning from the providers to the learners;
- cooperate to develop a global qualification system guaranteed by reliable quality assurance, and reflecting the principles of modularization and credit accumulation and transfer;
- promote the development of the LP;
- create incentives to encourage lifelong learning (eg by adjustments to taxation);
- ensure that appropriate programmes for lifelong learning are available, accessible to all without exclusion, and that diverse pathways to learning form a seamless curriculum;
- encourage the development of Cities of Learning and develop a system of recognition for these;
- cooperate to organize a world learning day;
- provide special support to families in disadvantaged circumstances to enable children to start right, and to encourage lifelong learning in the home.

7. The media should:
- mount a campaign to raise awareness of a chance of lifelong learning and encourage higher aspirations and expectations;
- support the learning process by demonstrating that learning is fun;
- develop regional learning channels on radio and television;
- provide local educational support programmes.

8. Those who organized and attended the Rome Conference should:
- commit themselves to the principles of lifelong learning set out in this report;
- support the World Initiative on Lifelong Learning in the championship of lifelong learning globally;
- develop regional structures including the establishment of a Central and East European Steering Committee for Lifelong Learning;
- create a recurrent two yearly conference on lifelong learning.

Notes

1 The essential features of a Learning Organization are set out in the introduction to this report.
2 Such targets should be benchmarked against best practice and include (a) an elementary target for functional literacy and numeracy, (b) a foundation target for school leaving proficiency (c) an advanced level target and a further level target for higher education for both young people and for mature adults, and (d) a target for Learning Organizations, together with target dates for achievement. Learning targets should be revised in the light of experience and progress.

The World Initiative on Lifelong Learning

The World Initiative on Lifelong Learning was founded by delegates at the First Global Conference on Lifelong Learning held in Rome in December 1994. It builds on the experience of the European Lifelong Learning Initiative (ELLI). Its council is chaired by John Towers MBE, Chief Executive of the Rover Group Ltd, and will contain members from industry, higher education, NGOs and government.

The World Initiative will set in motion a series of measures to establish a global infrastructure to promote fruitful dialogue, continuing development, the sharing of good practice and ideas, monitoring and measuring activities and the creation of standards for lifelong learning on a global basis. These measures will be achieved through the following.

Global Conferences *Second Global Conference on Lifelong Learning* Ottawa, Canada, 23–25 September 1996. *Third Global Conference on Lifelong Learning* planned for late 1998, Africa, Asia, South Pacific. *The Millennium Global Conference on Lifelong Learning* planned for late 2000, Europe.

Publications and journals *COMMENT*, distributed four times per year. *LifeLine*, a learned journal to be launched in late 1996. *BUSILearn*, for and about developments in Learning Organizations in industry and business.

WILLnet Global Networks A true world-class learning network on the Internet for delivery of information about learning to individuals.

Working groups Electronic debates on issues and solutions in the field of lifelong learning.

Issue seminars, workshops and conferences

WILLnets Regional groups of members for specific cultural and local issue development. Regional annual conferences.

Workshops and seminars International, national and by area. For and between all sectors.

Research projects Member collaboration on the top priority issues and action programmes for lifelong learning.

World development projects Global cooperation on 'world learning' matters.

WILL regions include North America, Africa, South America, Australasia, Latin America and Asia and Pacific Rim. National organizations may function independently or collaboratively within these regions.

The World Initiative on Lifelong Learning invites the participation of:

Business, industry and commerce – which is pioneering lifelong learning as a part of its survival strategy, but can improve immeasurably its performance and understanding when it cooperates with other sectors of society.

Higher education – which lies at the hub of local life in all sectors of activity. It is a natural place to initiate, develop and maintain lifelong learning programmes within its geographical area while also maintaining links with national and international projects and activities.

International, national and local government organizations – which play a leading role in providing vision, creating development opportunities and in setting and monitoring policies and standards for lifelong learning.

Professional associations and non-governmental organizations – which must keep themselves and others up to date and need to know how the concepts of lifelong learning can be applied within their own organizations and for the professional development of their members.

Schools and teacher training establishments – which, since lifelong learning begins in childhood, are crucial organizations for shaping those attitudes and values which prepare future adults for a world in which flexibility and adaptability are essential, and in which the enjoyment of learning may be a matter of personal survival.

Adult education organizations in the formal and informal education sectors – which provide learning opportunities in a wide range of subject areas.

Vocational education organizations – which influence the creation and maintenance of employability for the future and need to employ innovative strategies to do so.

And of course:

Individuals – who in the final analysis have to develop the personal values, skills and understandings which enable them to adapt to the world as it is and will become.

Many of the World Initiative's activities are based on the recommendations of the Action Agenda on Lifelong Learning, which highlights action to:

- create Learning Organizations

- develop skill profiles
- initiate individual lifetime learning plans
- make lifelong learning a major business process
- introduce the profession of learning counsellors
- provide learning opportunities in lifelong learning
- create a lifelong learning passport
- improve accessibility to learning
- increase the use of educational technology
- utilize networks, such as the Internet
- create better tools for measuring effective learning
- develop and monitor standards for learning materials and methods
- introduce targets for learning at all levels
- clarify roles of all stakeholders in the learning process
- accredit courses wherever they take place
- initiate portability in qualifications
- prioritize essential new research
- make learning a joy!

If ever we thought that lifelong learning could be implemented easily this (initial) task list should make us stop and think again. Everywhere, and for years to come, there is much to be done. It demands insight, wisdom, energy and commitment.

Interested people and organizations are invited to ring, fax or write to Lieve de Geest, Keith Davies or Norman Longworth at 60 Rue de la Concorde, 1050 Brussels. Tel: (322) 540 9752; Fax: (322) 514 1172.

Odyssey of the Mind

If values in lifelong learning are about developing the creative potential of human beings, the Odyssey of the Mind tournament is an excellent example of how a large number of children can be turned on to this way of thinking. Odyssey of the Mind is a friendly problem-solving competition for schools. Begun in 1978 between five schools in the USA, it has achieved such a status that now more than one million children from 12,000 schools in 18 countries have participated.

The finals, held in quasi-Olympic conditions to bring together young people, their teachers/coaches and sometimes their parents, were attended this year by 712 teams from Hungary, China, Japan, Lithuania, Russia, Kazakhstan, the UK, the Netherlands and most states of the USA. The competition takes place in four groups based on the age of the children, who are also invited to find 'unique', creative solutions to four different types of problems in each group, from the broad areas of:

Literature – in 1993 teams had eight minutes to create and present a performance based on Hemingway's *The Old Man and the Sea*. It included a parody or analogy of the true meaning of the book.

Science and technology – in 1993 teams had to design, build and drive a vehicle powered by one or two mechanical jacks – and present creative solutions to other problems related to the design.

Civil engineering – in 1993 teams designed and built a balsa wood structure to certain dimensions which would support as much weight as possible (the winners supported more than 500kg).

History – in 1993 teams had to create and present a story about dinosaurs including a team-made dinosaur and a new discovery – 'creativosaurus'.

Children design their own sets for the plays and construct their own artifacts. They must use everyday materials and not spend more than a preset limit to do so. Teams are of not more than seven people. At the finals a spontaneous creative event is also required of the teams in which they are given just two minutes to solve a presentation problem.

The enthusiasm of the children and the creative approaches to presentations and problem-solving need to be seen to be believed. It is a marvellous example of the power of cooperative effort within, and often between, teams. Though some teams get awards, there are no losers. In true Olympic fashion, participation is all.

Odyssey of the Mind is supported by industry and by national and local authorities in many states and countries. Each gains from the publicity which the event generates and from the enthusiastic commitment of the children who participate. Further details can be obtained from Robert T Purifico, Executive Director, OM Association Inc, PO Box 547, Glassboro, New Jersey 08028-0547, USA.

References and Further Reading

Adey, K (1995) 'Structural Imperatives in Lifelong Learning', in *International Symposium on Lifelong Learning and Extension at Educational Universities*, Asahikawa, pp 31–6.

Aulich, Senator T (Chair) (1990) *Priorities for Reform in Higher Education*, Report of the Senate Standing Committee on Employment, Education and Training, Australian Government Publishing Service, Canberra, p xiii.

Australian Higher Education Council (1992) *Higher Education: Achieving Quality*, Australian Government Publishing Service, Canberra.

Ball, C (1992) *Profitable Learning*, RSA, London.

Ball, C (1995) 'Learning Does Pay', in *Bringing Learning to Life: The Learning Revolution, The Economy and the Individual*, C A Bradshaw (ed), Falmer Press, London.

Ball, C and Stewart, D (1995) *An Action Agenda for Lifelong Learning for the 21st Century*, Report from the First Global Conference on Lifelong Learning, N Longworth (ed), World Initiative on Lifelong Learning, Brussels.

Bower, D Jane (1992) *Company and Campus Partnership*, Routledge, London.

Bradshaw, C A (ed) (1995) *Bringing Learning to Life: The Learning Revolution, the Economy and the Individual*, Falmer Press, London.

Candy, P, Crebert, G and O'Leary, J (1994) *Developing Lifelong Learners through Undergraduate Education*, Australian Government Publishing Service, Canberra.

Cann, T (1995) 'Structures and Funding', in *Bringing Learning to Life: The Learning Revolution, The Economy and the Individual*, C A Bradshaw (ed), Falmer Press, London.

Clarke, A C (1986) *Prelude to Space*, Ballantine, New York (First published in 1963).

Cochinaux, P and De Woot, P (1995) *Moving Towards a Learning Society*, A Forum Report by European Round Table of Industrialists (ERT) with Standing Conference of Rectors, Vice-Chancellors and Principals of European Universities (CRE), Brussels.

Comenius (Jan Amos Komensky) *Pampaedia*, A M O Dobbie (ed), Buckland, 1987.

Commission of the European Communities (1991a) *School and Industry – IRDAC Opinion*, Industrial Research and Development Advisory Committee of the Commission of the European Communities (IRDAC), Brussels.

Commission of the European Communities (1991b) *Skills for a Competitive and Cohesive Europe*, Commission of the European Communities, Brussels.

Commission of the European Communities (1991c) *Skills Shortages in Europe,* Industrial Reasearch and Development Advisory Committee of the Commission of the European Communities (IRDAC), Brussels.

Commission of the European Communities (1991d) *Vocational Training in the European Community in the 1990s,* Commission Memorandum TFRH/36/92-EN, Task Force Human Resources, Education, Training and Youth, Brussels.

Commission of the European Communities (1992a) *Concerning the Development of EC/US Cooperation in the Field of Education and Training,* Paper SEC (92) 1023 Final, Brussels.

Commission of the European Communities (1992b) *European Higher Education–Industry Cooperation: Advanced Training for Competitive Advantage,* Commission of the European Communities, Luxembourg.

Commission of the European Communities (1993) *Guidelines for Community Action in the Field of Education and Training,* Commission working paper COM (93) 183 Final, Brussels.

Diez-Hochleitner, R (1995) *Higher Education: Capacity Building for the 21st Century,* New papers on Higher Education No 6, pp 43–52, UNESCO, Paris.

Eurich, N (1985) *Corporate Classrooms. The Learning Business,* Carnegie Foundation for the Advancement of Teaching, New York.

European Round Table of Industrialists (ERT) (1989) *Education and European Competence,* ERT Education Policy Group, Brussels.

ERT (1992) *European Approaches to Lifelong Learning,* ERT Education Policy Group, Brussels.

ERT (1995) *Education and European Competence,* ERT Education Policy Group, Brussels.

Handy, C (1992) *Managing the Dream: The Learning Organisation,* Gemini Consulting Series on Leadership, London.

Handy, C (1995) *The Empty Raincoat,* Hutchinson, London.

Hobbs, J (1995) 'Report on Adult and Vocational Education Systems', in *Community Action for Lifelong Learning,* Part 2 of Report of the First Global Conference on Lifelong Learning, N Longworth and L de Geest (eds), pp 25–30, World Initiative on Lifelong Learning, Brussels.

International Labour Office (1986) *Vocational Training, Glossary of Selected Terms,* International Labour Office, Geneva.

Longworth, N (1976) 'Information Skills in Secondary Schools Curricula', MPhil thesis, School of Education, University of Southampton, Southampton.

Longworth, N (1980) *The Woodberry Down School/IBM Basinghall Street Twinning Scheme,* IBM United Kingdom Ltd, London.

Longworth, N (1983) 'Educating the Information Generation', Invited paper for IFIP World Conference on Computers in Education, Lausanne, *Information Processing 83,* North Holland, Amsterdam.

Longworth, N (1990) 'From Computing to Information Technology to Distance

Education – What do we do when Teacher isn't there?' Keynote paper at IFIP World Conference on Computers in Education, Sydney, published in *Proceedings of WCCE90*, North Holland, Amsterdam.

Longworth, N (1994) 'Lifelong Learning and the Community – Relations with Business and Industry, Towards a Holistic Mission', *New Papers on Higher Education No 6, UNESCO*, pp 211–12.

Longworth, N (1995a) 'Lifelong Learning: The Challenge and Potential for Higher Education and Industry', *Industry and Higher Education*, 9 (4), pp 205–14.

Longworth, N (1995b) 'The Challenge of Lifelong Learning for Educational Universities', in *International Symposium on Lifelong Learning and Extension at Educational Universities*, Asahikawa, pp 13–18.

Longworth, N and Beernaert, Y (eds) (1995) *Lifelong Learning in Schools*, European Lifelong Learning Initiative, Brussels.

Longworth, N and De Geest, L (eds) (1995) *Community Action for Lifelong Learning for Developing Human Potential*, Part 2 of Report of First Global Conference on Lifelong Learning, Rome, World Initiative on Lifelong Learning, Brussels.

Longworth, N and Gwyn, R (1989) 'The PLUTO International Networking Project', *European Journal of Education*, 24 (1), pp 79–84.

Marquardt, M (1995) 'Building a Global Learning Organisation', *Industry and Higher Education*, 9 (4), pp 217–26.

Musto, F (1989) 'Key Issues in Distance Education: An Industrial Viewpoint', *European Journal of Education*, 24 (1), pp 25–36.

Naisbitt, J (1985) *Megatrends*, Organization for Economic Cooperation and Development (OECD), Paris.

Naisbitt, J and Aburdine, P (1986) *Re-inventing the Corporation*, Futura, London.

Okamoto, K (1994) *Lifelong Learning in Japan*, OECD, Paris.

OECD (1994) *The OECD Jobs Study – Facts, Analysis, Strategies*, OECD, Paris.

OECD (1996) 'Making Lifelong Learning a Reality for All', Press release number 2803, OECD Press Division, Paris.

Otala, L (1993) 'Lifelong Learning of Engineers in Industry', *International Association for Continuing Education of Engineers (IACEE) report No 2/1993*, IACEE, Espoo.

Otala, L (1993) *Lifelong Learning Based on Industry–University Cooperation*, University of Technology Lifelong Learning Series 1/1993, Centre for Continuing Education, Espoo.

Oxtoby, B (1995) 'Report on Informal Education Systems, the Community and Non-Governmental Organizations', in *Community Action for Lifelong Learning*, Part 2 of Report of the First Global Conference on Lifelong Learning, N Longworth and L de Geest (eds) pp 50–56, World Initiative on Lifelong Learning, Brussels.

Plagemann, K-E (1994) 'Odyssey of the Mind: An International Competition in Creative Thinking and Acting', Berlin Brandenburgische Auslandsgesellschaft, Berlin.

Rover Learning Business (1994) *Learning Organisation* (booklet), Rover Learning Business, Birmingham.

Stahl, T, Nyhan, B and D'aloja, P (1993) *The Learning Organization: A Vision for Human Resource Development*, Commission of the European Communities, Brussels.

Stanford, B K (1993) *Fostering Lifelong Learning*, 2nd International Congress of Educating Cities, Gothenburg, Sweden, Department of Employment and TAFE, South Australia.

Stonier, T (1983) *The Wealth of Information*, Thames Methuen, London.

UNESCO/Club of Rome (1979) *No Limits to Learning*, UNESCO Publishing, Paris.

UNESCO Commission on Education for the 21st Century (1996), *Learning: The Treasure Within*, UNESCO, Publishing, Paris.

Verspoor, A (1991) 'The International Dimension of Higher Education – Perspectives Round Table', in *New Papers on Higher Education No 1*, UNESCO, Paris.

Index

INDEX